CW00501174

The Book Mill

MARGARET FORSTER
FORSTER
A Life in Books

KATHLEEN JONES

Kathleen Jones is a biographer and poet whose short stories have won several awards including a Cosmopolitan fiction prize and a Fay Weldon award. Kathleen's biography of Catherine Cookson was in the top 10 best-seller racks in WH Smith for 8 weeks. Her first novel, The Sun's Companion, was short-listed for the Kindle Review best historical novel of 2013. Born and brought up on a hill farm in the Lake District, Kathleen currently spends a lot of time in Italy with her partner, sculptor Neil Ferber and runs a creative writing course there every September. She is a Royal Literary Fund Fellow and, in 2012, was elected as a Fellow of the English Association.

Further information at: www.kathleenjones.co.uk

PREFACE

This short, critical biography was first commissioned by the Arts Council who thought it would be
interesting to have one northern author write about
another. I expected Margaret to hate the idea, but
she didn't. The only drawback was that she didn't
want to be interviewed. She was quite happy for me
to write about her work and share information that
was in the public domain, but she wanted to protect
her privacy. This was something I completely understood. Writing about a contemporary, especially
one with such a formidable reputation, is an ordeal,
without the added complications of delving into
deeply private lives. I gladly agreed. Margaret was
always willing to answer questions about her books;
her life was strictly off-limits. Although I knew about
her struggle with cancer I couldn't mention it in the
biography until she herself had gone public with it.
Her relapse was a closely guarded secret. I am not
one of those who believe that biographers and journalists have the right to expose the private lives of
individuals, while they are still living them. There
would have to be an overwhelming argument that
the publication of such material was for the public
good.

   Like Margaret, I was born and brought up in

Cumbria, from a working class background, and state educated. Quite a lot of my relatives lived in Carlisle as Margaret's family did. Although she was older than I was, the context of her life was familiar to me and it gave me an understanding of hers. But we were very different. As a teenager I, too, couldn't wait to get out of Cumbria, but disappointed my parents and teachers by not taking the Oxbridge route. I left school at sixteen and went off to London as soon as I could with the intention, like Margaret, of becoming a writer, but without the slightest idea how I was going to accomplish it. Margaret had a very clear vision of what she wanted her life to be - I hadn't a clue. She was confident and determined; I had no confidence at all, only an ambition.

Margaret was already an established writer when I was growing up and she was a big influence on me. The local girl from Carlisle who had become so famous made me believe it was possible for someone ordinary to become a published writer. But she had a formidable reputation. Intellectually rigorous and morally uncompromising, Margaret did not suffer fools of any kind and she dealt ruthlessly with the slightest whiff of pretention.

She had no time for euphemisms. A spade was very definitely a spade, and her honesty sometimes terrified other people. Even as she lay, terminally ill, in the hospice there was no talk of 'passing away', or 'kicking the bucket'; 'What's wrong with the word "dead"?' Margaret asked. And she ridiculed those who talked about her brave 'battle' with cancer. 'There is no fighting that can be done,' she observed.

'And being positive not only has no proven effect but it creates another psychological burden for the patient.' She saw the illness as a 'touch of woodworm, or dry rot' in the house of the body - an insidious invasion that might never properly be eradicated. It takes courage to see things with such ruthless clarity.

Margaret refused to compromise. Her life revolved around her family and her writing. She wasn't interested in the trappings of literary fame, though she did enjoy the financial benefits it brought. Publishers resigned themselves to the fact that she wouldn't go to literary festivals to promote her books. A little radio, a few magazine and newspaper articles, some photo-shoots and that had to be enough. Margaret didn't do literary dinner parties either and many thought her sharp-tongued and reclusive. As a new, rather self-conscious young writer, I was terrified of her reputation. I remember being struck dumb on a public platform where I was supposed to be giving a talk, because someone told me that Margaret was sitting in the back row of the audience. When I actually met her, on another occasion, I was so tongue-tied I could barely stammer 'hello'. She must have thought me a complete idiot.

But the friends who knew her well loved her incisive mind (Hunter Davies said that she was the most intelligent woman he had ever known) and she was extraordinarily generous. I certainly found her so. She gave my book '*A Passionate Sisterhood*' such a rave review, I still blush when I read it. When I asked for permission to re-write the short critical biography I had originally been commissioned by the Arts Council to write, to bring it up to date, she gave me un-qualified permission and her only worry was that it might cost me money, since she wasn't a sufficiently famous author (in her eyes) to merit such a work. But it wasn't a question of money, more of recognition for a Cumbrian writer I had always believed to be critically under-rated.

Her best work, in my opinion, is her memoir writing - *Hidden Lives* and *Precious Lives* - the stories of her own family. They reveal, more expertly than anything else I have ever read, the difficulties and tragedies, and the sheer waste of talent, of what used to be called 'the servant class' in the days before the welfare state, when women in particular were at the mercy of unscrupulous employers. As we slide towards social inequality once more, books like this are worth reading as an awful reminder of what happens when we lose health care and education as a basic human right.

When you write about a living author, they are constantly adding to the story. It was her husband, Hunter Davies who suggested that I should update the original Arts Council booklet. He had invited me to be a judge for a literary award he sponsored, the Lakeland Book of the Year Awards, presented at a big literary lunch. I served on the panel with Hunter and TV news reader Fiona Armstrong for several years. Margaret, of course, gave the whole thing a wide berth. But Hunter, too, felt that Margaret had not had the recognition she deserved and was very happy to encourage a more substantial critical biography.

Margaret Forster died on the 8th February, 2015

aged seventy-seven, and I have once again updated the book to take that into account. Margaret was a very special person and she will be much mourned by family, friends and readers alike.

~~~~~~~~~~~~~~~~~~~

MARGARET FORSTER

A Life in Books

Margaret Forster was one of the United Kingdom's most prolific writers. Since her first novel in 1964 she published a book almost every year, across five decades - a mixture of biography, memoir, social history and fiction that finds it way more surely to the literary sections of the bookshop than to the stacks of popular pulp. Margaret was not a 'romantic' author in the modern, pejorative, sense of the word - for fifty years in fiction and non-fiction, she explored the rich territory of family relationship - the tyranny of love and obligation that has provided the fabric of both tragedy and comedy for generations of literary ancestors.

There is always a lot to talk about in Margaret's Forster's work - her feisty heroines, her blend of fact and fiction, her uncompromising tone, her exploration of difficult contemporary issues. This is one reason why her books are often Book Group choices.

Her fiction is wholly unclassifiable. From her first 'provincial girl about town' novels through a succession of turbulent anti-heroines and a brief excursion into gothic romance (the *Bride of Lowther Fell*) to her more recent explorations of social issues and forays into 'faction', there is no recognisable 'Forster novel' in the way that one can identify a Mary Wesley, a Joanna Trollope or a Margaret Drabble. They are not romances, or aga-sagas, bodice-rippers, or 'clog and shawls', not regional novels such as those written by Cookson or du Maurier, nor has she produced the literary exam paper fodder of authors such as Margaret Atwood and Carol Shields.

Her work is understated and subtle, as a *Guardian* reviewer recently observed: 'like many female writers who have never quite got the recognition they deserve, she is an unassuming prose stylist. Her sentences are crafted with an artisanal eye - brief descriptions that never intrude; quietly powerful turns of phrase. Her plots take place in ordinary houses, on ordinary streets, within ordinary families.'[1]

If there is to be any classification at all it can only be that the subject matter of her novels is the family life of the contemporary, upwardly mobile, working and lower-middle classes, and the day to day issues that confront them. It's a universal subject. We are all part of one family or another and our experience of family life teaches us how the world works. As one historian wrote recently, 'kinship networks [are] a vital means of understanding power relations.'[2] Within this frame Margaret's work is ruthlessly honest. As one reviewer has put it, 'She is a chronicler of our cruel little ways within the family; she can be harsh; she gives no quarter whatsoever.'[3]

1

Margaret Forster was born in the northern city of Carlisle in 1938. Her family was firmly working class. Margaret's mother was a nervous, repressed woman who found daily life difficult to cope with and took refuge in religion; her father was stubborn, laconic, emotionally detached - a man who was not on speaking terms with his brother for all of thirty years. At the time of Margaret's birth he was a fitter at the Metal Box factory and they lived in a two bedroom council house on the outskirts of the city in the new estate of Raffles - then considered a model in urban regeneration, but which after the war became run-down and eventually notorious.

Margaret, named after her maternal grandmother, was the middle child and the most difficult of the three siblings. She admits that she was 'noisy and demanding and given to tantrums . . . Fiery, selfish, ambitious . . .' But precociously clever. Margaret was a child who 'talked in long sentences at two and never stopped asking questions and wanting to try to read.'[1] By the time she was four she could already do so and the local headmistress was so impressed she was admitted to the infants' class almost a year early.

Throughout her childhood Margaret witnessed her mother's response to the demands of her family, friends and neighbours, the sacrifice of self that left her exhausted and depressed, and soon came to the conclusion that her mother was trapped by the traditional domestic role accepted by generations of women. Long before feminism was a word in her vocabulary, Margaret resolved that she would never do the same. 'I would not marry and therefore would not have children. I would keep out of the trap and I'd be safe. . . The circumstances of my mother's life and her unhappiness were the spur to make my own life into something different. I would not and could not be like her.'[2] The way to escape, Margaret became convinced, was through education.

In *Hidden Lives*, Margaret's family memoir, she describes her own feelings of difference and the difficulties she found in fitting into the role her family expected of her. When her father accused her of trying to be something she wasn't, the eight year old Margaret was faced with the knowledge that she was not the child everyone thought she was; there was a secret self that defeated familial expectations. 'I wasn't . . . a nice little girl which is what my mother wanted me to be. I was by then already difficult, moody. I'd left behind that pretty little dear they'd all drooled over.'[3] School was the only place where that other self could emerge: 'I was bright-faced, eager, absolutely desperate to please.' Margaret's mother tried to impress on her daughter the traditional female values -

'I mustn't think being clever was as important
as being nice and good. She wanted a sweet,
kind, thoughtful, willing-to-help daughter

ready to follow in her footsteps in that respect. Instead I was already walking away
from this calling. I didn't want to learn to be
any kind of carer. I wouldn't accept that my
role as a female was to serve on the domestic
front. My father raged against my disobedi-
ence. I wouldn't wash dishes, set and clear
tables, bring the coal in, or in any other ways
help my mother.'[4]

Margaret was slapped and then strapped, but she
refused to submit, spending much of her time at a
friend's house. 'If I had to be at home I read my li-
brary books. I'd sit absorbed, hearing nothing, until
my father would snatch the book away and shout,
'Get your nose out of that book and help your mam,
or else!'[5]

At ten Margaret passed what was then called the
'Merit' exam (later known as the eleven plus) and
gained a coveted place at the Carlisle and County
High School for girls, where - driven by her thirst
for knowledge and her need to escape the confines of
her environment - she quickly excelled. Her parents
were both proud and anxious, fearful that Margaret
would get 'above herself' and become totally unfit for
what they saw as her role in life. She was being educated out of her class and away from her family. 'My
mother . . . saw it as creating that very gulf she dreaded. The more I read, the further away I grew.'[6] There
were few books at home - their titles predictable: the
Bible, prayer books, home medical encyclopaedias,
cookery books, a few children's books, no novels,

poetry or biography. There was no money for such things and even less interest.

> 'I could never discuss anything I'd read at home. Trying to talk about the contents of books was showing off and there was no need for it. My reading was seen as a weapon I used against my family, a way of absenting myself from their company. "All she does is that damned reading," my father complained, and it was true. It made me strange to them.'[7]

Margaret was undeterred. Everything she saw around her convinced her that she wanted a different life and that there was only one way to achieve it. 'The vital thing was to be independent, to be single-minded, to have a goal and allow no distractions.'[8] That goal had already been suggested by her teachers: university. And not just any university - it had to be Oxford or Cambridge. There were now grants for students whose parents couldn't afford the fees. In addition Margaret worked in Marks & Spencer on Saturdays and during the holidays either in the post office or at the steam laundry to earn extra money. Her experience of unskilled work made her even more determined. She didn't want what other women wanted, 'some kind of pleasant job for a few years until Mr Right came along. . .' Others viewed with hostility her need to escape what they saw as her natural destiny. 'To *want* so much, as I did, was to be hard and selfish and strange. It was not normal to be

18

so restless, to be so demanding. Aiming at Oxford or Cambridge was showing off. . . It was unsettling, disturbing . . .'[9]

~~~~~~~~~~~~~~~~~~~~

2

Ironically, by the time she was seventeen Margaret had already met the man she was to marry. Hunter Davies was, if not exactly the boy next door, very close to it. He was educated at the boys' grammar school in Carlisle, a scholarship boy with a similar working class background. Hunter and Margaret both went to the Garrett Club, which was a kind of youth club for fifth and sixth form students and Hunter described his attempts to get to know her in his short memoir of growing up in Carlisle, '*Strong Lad wanted for Strong Lass*'.

Their first meeting, at a Saturday night dance, wasn't a great success. Hunter saw her across the room.

> 'I already knew about her because she was said to be the High School's star pupil, a right blue-stocking. . . She looked attractive to me, so I thought I'd chance my arm and I asked her if she fancied a dance. "Certainly not," she said. "In fact there's nothing I would like less. I hate dancing . . ." And with that, she was off. Leaving the Garrett Club.' [1]

Hunter didn't talk to her again for almost two years, during which time he began studying at Durham University, but during one of the vacations when he was working as a bus conductor, Margaret got onto his bus and went to sit upstairs. 'Showing

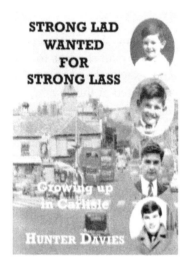

STRONG LAD
WANTED
FOR
STRONG LASS

Growing up
in Carlisle

HUNTER DAVIES

off, being Big Mick, trying to impress,' Hunter said he'd let her off the fare. But Margaret followed him down the stairs and insisted on paying for her ticket. 'She certainly wasn't going to be let off, cheating the system.' Margaret got off the bus without a backward glance.

A less courageous man might have been daunted, but Hunter was made of stronger stuff. Passing the cinema he saw Margaret and another girl standing in the queue with a couple of his old friends from school and decided on the spur of the moment to join them.

'I ended up in the row behind as the four of them had managed to sit together. This didn't put me off and during the film I kept up an inane conversation over their shoulders, trying to be smart and amusing.' When they came out of the cinema and were standing on the pavement chatting before going their separate ways home, Hunter suddenly found himself asking Margaret if he could walk her home and to his amazement she said yes. 'And that was it. I walked her home. It turned out to be a very long walk, one I am still walking.'[2]

They had shared aspirations. 'Together we wanted to escape the limits of our social background and gain what our city couldn't give us. We wanted to go in the same direction,'[3] Margaret wrote later. The relationship continued at long distance while Hunter attended Durham University and then got a job as a journalist in London, and then through Margaret's admission to Oxford to read History on an Open Scholarship. As neither had very much money, there was a great deal of hitch-hiking - mainly Hunter's - in order to see each other.

In her teens Margaret's rebellion against what was expected of her was in full flight. She wore the black clothes that would later be described as 'beatnik', cropped her hair unfashionably short, and refused to wear high heels and stockings. In nineteen-fifties Carlisle this made her an oddity, but she didn't care. Margaret revelled in her difference. All her sights were fixed on either Oxford or Cambridge and both invited her to interview. Margaret found Cambridge unappealing, but her interview at Oxford's Somerville College brought her into contact with the legendary Janet Vaughan whose background was quite similar to her own. Janet not only had working class origins, but had managed to combine a high-flying academic career with marriage and motherhood. She was just the sort of role model that Margaret needed. At this point in her life her ambitions had begun to crystallise and focus on writing. Margaret had already decided that she would become a biographer.

After all the anticipation, the reality of Somerville College was a great disappointment. 'It was oppressive, I hated it and I wasn't going to fit in.' Scholarship, the 'life of the mind' that Margaret had longed for as an alternative to female domestic drudgery, bored her. But Oxford brought, not only the knowledge of contraception that allowed sexual liberation, but contact with educated women who juggled homes, children and careers successfully. For the first time Margaret began to realise that 'if I earned enough money I, too, could have it all, I could enjoy every aspect of a woman's life if I found I wanted to.'[4]

Margaret used her experience of Oxford as the basis for her first published novel *Dames' Delight*. Morag is the first of Margaret's spiky, rebellious, 'in-your-face' heroines. Like her author, Morag is a working class girl from a council house in Carlisle who wants to escape the existence she despises. The reality of Oxford is a shock. Morag's first evening in college is completely the opposite of what she had expected.

dames'
delight

MARGARET FORSTER

'Marvellously funny' — *Tes Tatler*
'Fresh and amusing' — *Sphere*

'I thought I'd never seen a more revolting sight than all those crowded tables full of jabbering excited females. They were so ugly. I went from face to face and felt more and more depressed. . . The sight of the high table distressed me even more. These were the Dons who were going to be my new masters, or so I imagined, and I felt I had to take their measure quickly. When they got up at the end of the meal they all walked as though their knickers were about to fall down, with their hands hunched protectively somewhere in the region of their navels.'[5]

As a northern girl, used to straight talking and a direct approach, Morag finds the oblique tact and the avoidance of issues frustrating. Original thought is not encouraged in tutorials.

> 'She had got on to books and happened to mention one awful one which I had actually read. Naturally, I sat up at that and said eagerly that I'd read it and she said what did I think of it? "Terrible," I said, "as dry as dust." There was a long silence. . . the atmosphere of outraged disapproval had penetrated even my thick skin. I began to feel more and more miserable as I saw what I had let myself in for. What did I care about history anyway? I hadn't a scholarly bone in my body.'[6]

Seeing her own image in a mirror in her scholar's gown, Morag stops to take a closer look. 'The gown was incongruous. There was I, frivolous, flippant and caring more about how long it took me to set my hair than how long it took to do an essay.' Like Margaret, Morag doesn't really fit in. She despises the other students especially:

> 'The type with the flat chest and rabbit chin who blushed when we had male butlers for big dinners (young women with the voices of forty or fifty). . . It was discouraging. Everybody wary of everybody else and finding refuge in keeping their distance so that they ended up howling with loneliness. . .'[7]

The men disgust her as well as the women. Morag goes to a Union debate and is outraged at 'the general idiocy so proudly displayed. It was a terrible thought that this lot was going to occupy the benches of the House of Commons in much the same way as they did that place. They cat-called each other all the way through and spent a lot of time banging their feet on the floor. And they did it all with such glee, as though it was only right and proper that the hall should be made a nursery.'[8]

The sexual freedom Morag sees around her doesn't appeal to her strong northern values either. 'I am sickened by all this emphasis on sex.' Morag seethes at the petty rules imposed on young women as though they were children - more constricting than living at home: men not allowed in college after seven, everyone in by twelve. She discovers that although she is clever she is not intellectual, preferring the *Express* to the *Guardian*. 'You've got to start doing something,' her friend Tom says. 'Such as what?' Morag asks. 'Act,' Tom says, 'write, or go into politics.' It was what Oxford graduates did.[9]

When Morag passes her preliminary exams, despite not really trying, she is shocked to find that she has achieved a distinction. She feels a fraud. 'I was reflecting that even in the exam field Oxford was dead phoney. A distinction, after that tripe.' Her tutor asks her if she is happy at Oxford. 'I hate it,' Morag admits bluntly. 'Anything I ever had before I came, Oxford has taken away. Like enthusiasm.' Morag falters because she knows the woman won't understand. 'The place stank, but I couldn't put my finger on why. . .' She decides to tolerate it for the two more years it will take to obtain her degree. '. . . what else was there to do? Theoretically, two years of living at other people's expense in a state of permanent leisure ought to have been idyllic. If I couldn't enjoy that, what was I going to enjoy, for God's sake?'[10]

~~~~~~~~~~~~~~~~~~~~

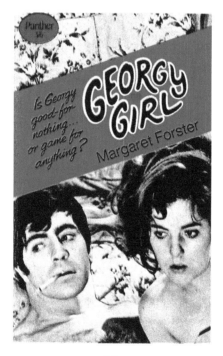

3

Hunter was afraid that once Margaret went to Oxford, 'mixing with the cream of the nation's youth',[1] their relationship would end. During her time at university Margaret met a much wider selection of men than she had been used to at home in Carlisle, including future playwright Dennis Potter with whom she performed in a production of the *Caucasian Chalk Circle*. He wrote to Margaret years later, in 1977, telling her that he had been in love with her and confessing how jealous he had been of Hunter Davies. 'I wrote back and told him he was talking rubbish,' Margaret said briskly.[2] None of the men she met caused her to rethink her first choice. By the time she left Oxford, Margaret had made two major decisions. She was going to marry Hunter Davies and she was going to give herself time to write a novel rather than a biography.

Aware that by marrying she was conforming to the very template she had treated with such scorn, Margaret made sure that her wedding made as few concessions to tradition as possible. A register office marriage with only two witnesses, no parents present, no bridesmaids, dresses, reception or any of the other trimmings. Her parents were horrified - she was letting them down, first by getting married, 'throwing herself and her education away' and then by having such a 'hole-and-corner' ceremony. Register offices were for divorcees and shotgun weddings. Hunter's family didn't approve of his choice either; Hunter's mother didn't get on with Margaret initially, finding her too outspoken, and his sisters made fun of her. But, sure of their own minds, Margaret and Hunter ignored the feelings of both the Forster and the Davies families.

The couple rented a flat in Hampstead and Margaret got a post as a supply teacher at schools in Paddington and Islington while Hunter began work as a journalist on the *Sunday Times* and, during the long summer vacation, she wrote her first novel *Green Dusk for Dream* which was promptly rejected by the agent she sent it to. Undaunted, Margaret put it in the bin and began *Dames' Delight*, writing in the evenings and at the weekends while she continued teaching. 'It wasn't a good novel but at least it got me started.'[3] Its acceptance gave Margaret the courage to stop teaching and turn to writing as a career.

Margaret and Hunter bought a run-down Victorian house on the 'wrong side' of Hampstead Heath and moved out of their rented flat. The new house was in Boscastle Road and needed complete renovation. It also had a sitting tenant on the top floor. But house prices in London, particularly Hampstead, were already rising and this 'wreck' - as Margaret described it - was all they could afford, even with a substantial mortgage. At the time it was going to be a temporary move, a stepping stone to their 'real' home, in one of the houses Margaret dreamed of, near the Heath. It was in Boscastle Road, in 1964, surrounded by building work and decorators, that Margaret wrote her second published novel, *Georgy Girl*, while pregnant with her first child.

Georgy Girl hit a nerve. Three young single people sharing a flat in London - their rebellion against parental values, their liberated sexuality - it was all on the front edge of the sixties' revolution. The novel is pacey and plot driven and there's some good writing: -

'It was a vicious, wet Sunday. By eleven o'clock it hardly seemed light at all, and the grey thickness of the rain clawed imploringly at the window panes. The square was deathly quiet, no traffic, no passers-by, it was sealed off. From one corner emerged Peg, with a pack-a-mac over her gaberdine and an umbrella held stiffly and vertically overhead. Like a smudge on a radar screen, she thumped across the square and up the steps to Number Seventeen.' [4]

Meredith Jones is another of Margaret's spiky heroines who refuse to conform to expectations and embrace traditional female values. Meredith's flatmate George is her antithesis - not particularly attractive physically, but affectionate and homely. Much of the dramatic tension in the novel is between these two female types. Meredith's boyfriend actually prefers George and when Meredith has a baby it is George who looks after it. Families aren't born, the author seems to say; a 'created' family can function better than a genetic one. Margaret Forster herself, firmly believed that 'an adoptive mother can be better than a real one'.[5] Unloving parents are a feature of the novel. George's 'real' parents, Ted and Doris, are very distant, lavishing more care and attention on their employer James and his beautiful house than they do on their daughter. They are better parents to James than they are to George. The 'real' parents of Meredith's baby, Sara, don't want her at all. They go off and leave her with George, who has come to 'adore and think and live and breathe' their baby.

> 'Really, she hadn't guessed how she would react to Sara either, even though she had thought so much about her. She had never imagined love for a baby, especially a baby that wasn't yours, could be so strong and emotional. When she'd held her for the first time, there was a physical sensation not unlike one of desire. The same weak feeling in her stomach, the same breathless anticipation.'

In a neat conclusion George marries James, even though she isn't in love with him because she knows he will provide the security she needs to blossom and a home for the baby she's adopted. Her parents are given the sack without a twinge of guilt, and sent out into the world to fend for themselves.

Later, looking back, Margaret observed that *Georgy Girl* wasn't the novel she had really wanted to write, and that it was now 'like an albatross round my neck'.[6] She also 'regretted' *Dames Delight* 'now mercifully out of print'. Her first and second novels had been a 'sulky reaction' to the rejection of her first book which she had hoped was going to be 'in the footsteps' of Balzac and Dickens, 'the sort of fiction I liked ... It took me eight more novels and ten years to get myself on the road that I should have been on all along.'[7]

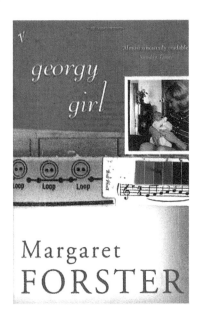

Dysfunctional parenting is also the subject of Margaret's third novel, published in the same year as her second, and it may be a re-write of her rejected first novel. If so, it's easy to see why her publishers didn't like it and it has remained one of her least popular books. *The Bogeyman* is now very hard to get hold of. Written with her first child Caitlin watching in the high chair and a film contract for *Georgy Girl* already under negotiation, the content of the novel is a savage indictment of familial relationships. Rather weaker than the first two in terms of character and plot, it is a very dark book. There is a sadistic, bad-tempered father (the bogeyman of the title), a weak and ineffectual mother and two cold and appallingly unattractive children. There isn't a single sympathetic person in the book, apart from the *au pair* whose arrival precipitates the family's destruction. There is violence and abuse, both physical and emotional, on almost every page. The faint ray of hope offered to the reader in the last chapter is scarcely credible in the light of what has gone before.

~~~~~~~~~~~~~~~~~~~~

4

Themes run through these first three novels that Margaret was to return to again and again - dysfunctional families, and difficult, non-conforming heroines who have bad relationships with their parents. The fathers in these stories are emotionally detached from their families and treated with indifference, contempt or straight-forward hatred. The reader is almost bound to speculate that Margaret's own insistence that she did not love her father informs their portrayal. Her adolescent clashes with him - both parties stubborn and outspoken - are analysed with brutal honesty in the second of her family memoirs, *Precious Lives*, written in 1998 after his death.

As a mature woman and successful author, their roles reversed, Margaret found herself motivated by duty and gratitude towards her father rather than love. Living at a distance she is thankful that she can hand the care of him over to others. At ninety-five he is still prejudiced, dictatorial and ferociously independent, but his carers are amused rather than repelled by him. 'What a character!' they exclaim and one of them asks 'What was he like when you were young?'

'He was a nightmare,' Margaret remembers. 'My appearance, while I was growing up was endlessly commented on and always critically. I was getting fat . . . my hair looked as if a mouse had chewed it . . . my spots were all barnacles . . .' Worst of all, for a self-conscious teenager, was the endless criticism of her clothes. 'Why didn't I wear nice frocks/high heels/nylon stockings/a decent coat?' Margaret realises that his insulting personal remarks have no power to hurt these unrelated women. 'The closer he got to dying the more outrageous he could be and they would go on admiring his spirit.'[1]

But in 1965, even with all the distance between London and Carlisle, Margaret was still struggling to get her father into perspective. Her mother was less difficult to understand. With the birth of her first child Margaret found herself faced with the same female dilemmas her mother had wrestled with. Career or family? Her mother had regretfully given up a job she loved to look after her husband and family and now in old age bemoaned the fact that she had done nothing with her life. Having her own home and a child made Margaret understand her mother better and realise how much they had in common.

Margaret also realised how lucky she was - writing was the ideal career to combine with a family; 'any career taking me out of the house would be unmanageable. It would present impossible choices, impose unacceptable strains. It would show I was, when it came to the crunch, exactly like my mother and grandmother; family first, no argument.' But like other women before her, Margaret found that, 'Being a wife, mother and writer was a balancing act.'[2]

One of the stipulations in Margaret's contract for

the film rights of *Georgy Girl* was that she write the film script - something she had no experience of at all, and she was also four months pregnant with her second child, Jake. Though Margaret made a start, it quickly became apparent that this kind of writing made a lot of professional demands she wasn't prepared for. 'One thing writing for myself, at home, quite another writing to orders, other people's orders . . . How clearly this episode showed me the limits of my own energies. Being a novelist fitted in with motherhood, being a scriptwriter didn't.[3] With great relief, Margaret handed the job over to Peter Nicholls, whose name appeared in the credits alongside her own, and went back to writing novels - this time with two small children underfoot.

When Caitlin was joined by a small brother, Jake, Margaret found it more difficult to write with two children, but she still refused to consider domestic help. 'I liked to do everything myself. I enjoyed the routine housework everyone else seemed to find odious.' Instead of an au pair Hunter and Margaret juggled domestic obligations. Two evenings a week Hunter bathed the children and put them to bed. Monday was his day off and so he took charge while Margaret wrote.

After *Georgy Girl*, she wrote two novels 'very quickly, both light affairs but acceptable enough. I was fond of saying it was like knitting, really, just something I did to amuse myself, quite effortless.'[4] If this is true, it is exceptional. Most writers struggle with some aspect of the creative process. But it was at this point, after five popular novels and a film deal, that Margaret's career as a writer seemed assured, though her parents remained doubtful. For Margaret's mother it wasn't a 'proper job' like teaching, more a kind of lucrative hobby which would surely have to be given up as the demands of her family increased.

While *Georgy Girl* was being filmed, Hunter also sold the film rights of his own novel, *Here we go, Round the Mulberry Bush*. Then he was commissioned to write a biography of the Beatles. Large sums of money, for the early nineteen sixties, were suddenly involved and, as income tax at the time was 95% for anyone earning more than a basic amount, Margaret and Hunter were advised to spend a year in tax exile. They reluctantly agreed, fearing that they might never earn this kind of money again. Hunter was granted a year's leave from the *Sunday Times* and they rented out their home in Boscastle Road.

They went first to Malta, which proved to be a mistake. Their house was a long way from the beach, it was hot and they both struggled to write. On the recommendation of a friend they moved to Portugal, to Praia da Luz - not yet developed into a resort - and rented a house with a big garden, near the sea. Hunter and Margaret took it in turns to take the children to the beach. Whichever one remained behind had time and solitude to write. They both discovered that they loved the Algarve and, before they left, bought a small house further up the coast to use as a holiday home.

Returning to London after fourteen months of enforced exile was a relief - the atmosphere of endless holiday had palled. There was a lack of the stimuli that both writers needed for their work.

~~~~~~~~~~~~~~~~~~~~

Margaret Forster
author of Georgy Girl

the travels of
maudie tipstaff

5

The Travels of Maudie Tipstaff, published in 1967, is a remarkable novel for a young woman of twenty-eight to write. Margaret manages to get right inside the head of Maudie, a puritanical, working class, elderly Glaswegian, unable to show love and affection to anyone over the age of nine and resolutely determined not to need it herself. Alone and abandoned at sixty-eight she sets out on a tour of duty round her three, very different, children. It's the first time she's been outside Glasgow; the first time she's had real contact with her children since they left home. Her expectations are based on weekly letters and her own imagined picture of her children's lives.

The result is disappointment and, as Maudie becomes aware of her failure to communicate with her children, and theirs with her, she begins to realise that she is trapped behind the barricades she has erected against human emotion. What she had valued as independence is really only a stubborn refusal to engage. This determined separateness is thrown into relief by having to be part of a family again: 'By herself, she was lonely, but with her children she was isolated.'

Maudie's visits are as difficult for her children as they are for her. 'Are there any happy families, do you think?'[1] one of the characters asks. Maudie changes their lives and becomes subtly changed herself. She realises that she must not expect anything from others, even her children, because in the end,

> 'everyone was on their own. . . Even when you had been physically joined to someone you were on your own, and even when you had created someone they were not an extension of yourself but someone separate, on their own. . . It made it more bearable to realise that her search had been fruitless before it began, because everyone was on their own.'[2]

Maudie turns this bleak message into a kind of triumph and returns home stronger and rather more human than she had been when she set out.

In the novel Margaret explores with great tact the difficulties of the middle class children of working class parents - the strange social shift made possible by free education, contraception and the vibrant sixties economic boom - a process she herself had been part of. Margaret's best novels are all rooted in fact. One of the things that most fascinates me, as a reader, is the way a writer transposes fact into fiction - actual experience and observation into art. For no work of fiction is entirely imagined - writers are thieves - they steal other peoples lives and stitch them into their own work.

In *The Travels of Maudie Tipstaff* Margaret used her memories of the elderly lodger, Mrs Hall, who occupied the top floor flat in the first house Margaret and Hunter owned after they were married, as well as Margaret's experiences of maintaining a relationship with her own parents and her Scottish mother-in-law. Maudie pays a visit to a small island near Malta, where Margaret and Hunter spent part of their tax exile, and the narrative owes much to visits made by their parents - who, like most working class people of that generation, had rarely had holidays and had never been abroad. Margaret felt sorry for her mother's inability to remove her clothing in the heat, even on the beach, suffering in the Mediterranean summer sun encased in corsets and stockings, petticoats and cardigans. Maudie, on a similar excursion 'already sweating in best coat and dress and laced shoes,' has to be accompanied by essentials such as 'umbrella, gloves, smelling salts, purse, handbag, cough sweets, watch. . .'[3]

In 1966, the year before the new novel was published, *Georgy Girl* was shown in the cinemas starring Lynn Redgrave. The film was a hit and Margaret suddenly became a 'name' in fiction. *Maudie Tipstaff* benefited from the publicity. 'Author of *Georgy Girl*' was printed on the cover and it rapidly became a book club choice. Margaret's future was assured. She was able to afford a second home in Cumbria, buy her parents the bungalow they had always longed to own and concentrate on writing with the knowledge that she was financially secure.

A clutch of books followed at yearly intervals. The novels - *The Park* (1968), *Miss Owen-Owen is at Home* (1969), *Fenella Phizackerley* (1970), *Mr Bones Re-*

treat (1971) and *The Seduction of Mrs Pendlebury* (1974) - all have certain features in common. Their heroines are feisty, prickly, unlikeable women - either physically unattractive (*Miss Owen-Owen*), or unnaturally

beautiful (*Fenella Phizackerley*). Mrs Pendlebury is an older woman - reclusive, difficult, neurotic. Damaged by a tragic incident in her past she has withdrawn from human contact and is - almost - rescued by the seductive wiles of a small child who lives next door. But there is no happy ending, no salvation for her. The snobbish, determined Miss Owen-Owen is similarly incapable of alteration, though Fenella Phizackerley does achieve happiness of a kind.

The Park was a departure from the usual narrative form, focussing on a group of unconnected women who walk regularly in the park during the day. Their lives run in parallel until a tragedy brings them all together. But once again the main female character is a managing, rather unpleasant personality. Bolshy women who refuse to fit into stereotypes had become Margaret Forster's speciality.

~~~~~~~~~~~~~~~~~~~~

6

During this period, Margaret wrote her first biography - *The Rash Adventurer* (1973) which is an account of the life of 'Bonnie Prince Charlie', also known as 'the Young Pretender', unfortunate Stuart heir to the thrones of England and Scotland. Having told Janet Vaughan during her Oxford interview that she wanted to be a biographer, it had taken Margaret sixteen years and eight novels to get there. Her biographies are as readable as her novels, with a strong narrative line - not scholarly compendiums bulging with irrelevant detail. There are some who might say that they are a little 'safe' and do not always ask the hard questions, but a biography does not have to be controversial to be good, and her scholarship is unimpeachable.

Her first choice of subject was interesting. Prince Charles Edward Stuart, grandson of the Catholic James II who had been forced to flee to France in 1688, was something of a local hero in Cumbria. He had stayed at the George Hotel in Penrith and the nearby Battle of Clifton Moor was the last ever fought on English soil. In 1745 many people in the north still harboured Jacobite sympathies and paid dearly for their part in the rebellion against the protestant Hanoverian George II, now comfortably occupying the throne of England. Further south it was a different story. Although Charles got as far as Derby, there was no popular rising to support him and the French failed to mount a diversionary invasion. Outnumbered, far into enemy territory, withdrawal to Carlisle was the only option his Scottish generals would consider. The Duke of Cumberland (nicknamed the Butcher) pursued them. Contemporary Cumbrian memoirs record the retreat, as Charles' soldiers were hounded back toward the Scottish border, and the River Eden was thick with floating bodies.

It was the consequence of another mismanaged, misjudged attempt to reclaim the crown for the Stuart dynasty. Attempts to re-instate James II had failed (notably at the Battle of the Boyne) and his son, 'the Old Pretender', had also made several botched efforts to invade England with French support. But the family refused to give up hope of sitting on the throne. Various European monarchs lent them support for devious reasons to do with their own struggles in the shifting landscape of European politics. The Stuarts became inconvenient guests and political pawns manipulated by the Pope, and the French and Spanish Kings.

Margaret was 'far from being obsessed' by the Jacobites. But she found their situation interesting, particularly that of Charles. 'Here was a man groomed for stardom who performed in blazing limelight for two short years and then was yanked off the stage protesting all the way. What does this kind of rejection do to a man?'[1] All the books previously written about Charles had focussed on the rebellion and his romanticised flight from Scotland aided by Flora Mc-Donald. But he had lived for another forty-two years and it was this period of his life that fascinated Margaret.

She began her research by asking where she should apply for permission to read his letters and papers, which are held in the Royal Archives at Windsor Castle. 'What followed was an object lesson of several kinds.' Margaret was discouraged from applying for permission from the Queen since, she was assured, it would only end in disappointment. '. . . it emerged that there really was a rigid rule that nobody got to see those papers without having written two works of historical value and without references from a couple of bishops and assorted ilk.' As an Oxford graduate and acclaimed novelist, Margaret found this 'shattering'. It seemed unfair that papers of such importance should be withheld. 'At a time when files only thirty years old are being opened for inspection at the Public Record Office, how can access to papers two hundred years old be made so difficult?' It particularly annoyed Margaret to find out that the Queen had shown some of Bonnie Prince Charlie's letters to guests at a cocktail party 'who probably wouldn't have known them from the Highway Code.' In the end she worked from poor quality micro-films, made during the war, developing a squint which 'I swear will be with me forever.'[2]

It's a novelist's biography rather than a historian's. There's a relish for character and 'story', rather than just the dry listing of historical and biographical detail. 'I wanted to write about Charles Edward, not

Jacobite history. It is his dilemma as a man, not his place in history, that attracts me.'[3]

Margaret came to 'respect and deeply admire' the historians whose work she read, and worked hard to avoid the traps laid out for any historical biographer - the temptations of 'academic bitchery', and the lure of romantic corruption. Her work is always rooted in fact and she avoids the dreaded 'must haves' that stalk all biographers faced with blank spaces in the record.

The psychological profile she constructs is a fascinating one. Charles Stuart's fate was mapped out for him from the very beginning. He 'was conceived and born for a definite purpose: to inherit the throne of England.'[4] Since this throne was already occupied by German George, this had an unfortunate influence on his character. Margaret portrays him as a 'rash adventurer' rather than a romantic figure - Bonnie Prince Charlie he is not. Charles could be guilty of 'staggering conceit, condescending, patronising and utterly lacking in any appreciation of either what had happened or was now happening'. When he led the ill-conceived rebellion that had such devastating consequences for the Highland Scots, he was apparently 'in the grip of a giant illusion . . . Nothing was his fault.'[5]

After Culloden, while poor, wounded, hungry Highlanders were turned away from people's doorsteps and left to starve or die of exposure, Charles would be reluctantly taken in and given aid. Margaret gives a clear picture of a situation where therewas one law for the rich, another for the poor and

49

dispossessed. Little thought was given by Charles to the fate of those who helped him - people were later arrested and persecuted - some even lost their lives. Margaret has little sympathy for the Prince's behaviour. When told of the suffering, massacres and devastation inflicted on the Highlands in retribution for his actions, 'It never for one moment made him think that enough was enough; all it did was harden his resolution to get back to France and start again.' Charles, apparently, still saw himself as a Deliverer and failed to acknowledge what had been plain - that the population were by no means on his side. Even when he changed his religion and declared himself to be a Protestant, no-one liked him any better for it, publicly or privately.

His character was far from likeable. Charles drank too much and got into violent disputes. He beat and ill-treated his Scottish mistress Clementina, mother of his only child, so badly that she escaped to a convent 'in fear of my life'. No woman, she wrote in the letter she left behind, would have suffered his behaviour as long as she had done. This proved to be true. He assaulted his young wife Louise so brutally she also took refuge in a convent. Other relationships were just as fraught. Charles had a difficult relationship with his father James, the Old Pretender, refusing to visit him when he was ill and leaving him to die alone. Charles didn't even make the funeral.

Yet Margaret manages to conjure up some sympathy for the man 'born to be king' whose character had been warped by other people's hopes and expectations. She comments on 'the sterility of his emotional life' and there's a hint that he might have been more interested in men than in women. As a young man it was a matter of note that he didn't take mistresses and never went whoring. He apparently lost his virginity to a woman at the late age of twenty-seven and didn't marry until he was fifty-two. There was only one child, a daughter, from whom he was estranged for most of her life. Of the three women he was involved with - two mistresses and a wife - the relationships were marred by violence.

Charles survived for forty-two years after Culloden - living on Patronage with the air of one who believes the world owes him a living. He was arrogant, spendthrift, always in debt, and sometimes a fugitive. Not only did he spend months living rough in the Highlands, he lived in disguise in Paris because the French king had banned him from the city.

There are no notes to this biography - only chapter bibliographies which make the book of less value to researchers and students. Margaret justifies her decision in a note at the end. 'This is not meant to be a work of reference, nor an original thesis, and I felt that as long as any interested reader was shown, in general, where to find the material I found, that was sufficient.'[6] But the lack of references is a pity.

Margaret's biography was well-timed. Antonia Fraser (who, as the daughter of Lord Longford and the biographer Elizabeth Longford, didn't have the same problems of access to royal archives) had recently had a best-seller with *Mary Queen of Scots* and interest in Mary's dispossessed descendant - a similarly romantic figure - was still strong. The styles of the two authors could not be more different - Antonia Fraser the 'portmanteau' school of historical biography, cramming every detail in; Margaret Forster's focus on the narrative and the evolution of character.

In publishing there is a long delay between finishing a book and seeing it in the bookshops. *The Rash Adventurer* had been completed in 1972 shortly before the birth of Margaret's third child, Flora, in October. Although Caitlin and Jake were now at school, the arrival of a third child changed the dynamics of Margaret's working life. 'There was little time for writing,' she admitted. 'I was too tired to even think of lifting a pen.'[7] The baby and the management of the house occupied a lot of time during the day and there were children to take to school and collect again, often with friends for tea, then dinner to cook and a husband home from work in the evenings. Most women writers with families will recognise the dilemma. Margaret was by now earning enough to buy in domestic help, but still refused to have more than occasional help with the cleaning. However, despite battling to find 'scraps of time'[8] in which to write, Margaret managed to finish *The Seduction of Mrs Pendlebury*, working for one precious hour in the morning while the baby slept.

The Rash Adventurer was published in 1973 and *The Seduction of Mrs Pendlebury* in 1974. But shortly afterwards, as she contemplated what she wanted to write next, Margaret discovered a small lump in her breast. It was a shock. She had no symptoms of cancer, was only thirty six, very fit, a non-smoker and had breastfed all her three children. In 1975 the treatment for even a small lump entailed the complete removal of the affected breast. Margaret's surgeon, the brusque Miss George, assured her that radiotherapy wouldn't be necessary as the cancer hadn't spread and the mastectomy had removed the tumour. For a young woman in her thirties with three children under the age of eight the diagnosis was terrifying. Flora was only two and a half years old. Margaret was told that it was just 'bad luck'.

Back in her own home in Boscastle Road, Margaret began to heal. She had discovered that cancer affected both mind and body and, although the body was treated, the mind was not. The conversations she overheard at the cancer clinic she regularly attended for check-ups, affected her deeply. She listened to the other women sharing their experiences, complaining that no-one talked to them or answered their questions. They were bewildered, resentful and afraid. 'Clinic days in the seventies were bad days'.[9] A few years later, some of these conversations would find their way into a novel, *Is There Anything You Want?* Margaret herself felt the anxiety of every cancer patient, unable to forget, particularly with a mastectomy scar as a constant reminder, checking and re-checking for recurring lumps, and living with fear.

Throughout this period Margaret was still finding time to write. She even wrote in her hospital bed, though forbidden by the nurses to use her favourite Waterman fountain pen. According to her friend, the author Valerie Grove, she briefly considered writing a novel 'about a woman who was the rock of her family (like her) being destabilised by cancer'. That novel was never written because Margaret didn't want to become known as 'a cancer survivor'. Her illness, and the trauma it caused, remained a private story.

She began working on a literary biography that was not in fact a true biography at all. *Thackeray*, listed variously under biography and memoir, 'edited' by Margaret Forster, should more accurately be described as a fictional autobiography. The jacket blurb describes how the book came about.

'William Makepeace Thackeray was once so disgusted by an unduly fulsome biography he was reading that he threw away the volume and said to his daughters, "Let there be none of this when I go." They saw to it that there was not. Yet what an autobiography this most witty and self-aware of Victorians could have written if he had chosen. Regretting that he had not, Margaret Forster decided, after reading every word he had ever written, she would let Thackeray speak for himself. The result is one of the most imaginative literary creations of modern times.'

Margaret took her cue from Thackeray himself in a lecture where he placed fictional portrayal in a finer light than biographical representation. 'Out of the fictitious book I get the expression of the life of the time; of the manner, of the movement, the dress, the pleasure, the laughter, the ridicule of society - the old times live again, and I travel in the old country of England.'[10]   Margaret became convinced that this was the way to do it. Thackeray should be allowed 'to write his own life using the very full published private papers together with the rich manuscript sources'. The result would be a biased account of the writer's life, but Margaret was happy to abandon the supposed objectivity of the biographer. 'I had no desire whatsoever to know how far Thackeray was telling the truth about himself.' How much of the text is quotation from Thackeray and how much Margaret's paraphrase is delicately glossed over.

'Would I paraphrase Thackeray's own writings? Decidedly not - and yet I knew it would be quite impossible not to use his actual words when they sprang unbidden to my pen. Should I therefore erase them, or acknowledge them? I have done neither. To anyone who knows their Thackeray the phrases will leap out of the page. To those who do not, it is my fond hope they will be indistinguishable. I see nothing immoral in this method. . . It is of course impertinent of me to presume I can write in the style of Thackeray . . . [But] . . . I believe Thackeray would have been amused by my impertinence. . . It might have made a better book to have approached Thackeray's life from every angle, but it would not have been such fun and to all those who may say this is neither one thing nor the other - neither fiction nor fact - I would say with Thackeray that it is through fiction we get our fact and that there is precious little fact that, when closely examined, is indisputably fact.'[11]

Margaret Forster added that she had 'never enjoyed writing anything as much as I have enjoyed writing this'. But I did not find it an easy book to read, nor Thackeray as amusing a person as Margaret would have liked me to, and I found myself longing for some objective commentary, or biographical illumination towards his relationships. This, for me, was not a successful foray into the twilight world of faction. Reviewers too found it almost impossible to categorise. It was published in 1978 - four years after her last book, *The Seduction of Mrs Pendlebury*, in 1974. Readers were totally unaware of the reason for this long gap.

~~~~~~~~~~~~~~~~~~~~

7

In January 1978 Margaret had a second mastectomy after a lump was detected in her remaining breast. The cancer cells had also spread to the lymph nodes. She was devastated. This time her cancer was treated more radically with radiotherapy and chemotherapy, but throughout all the biopsies, scans and other intrusive interventions Margaret maintained her northern stoicism. It was the family tradition to keep a stiff upper lip, but Margaret admitted that, 'It was harder, much harder to adjust this time'.[1] She was treated at the Royal Marsden Hospital, in a ward that contained several terminally ill patients. A woman with a brain tumour screamed with pain during the night and a priest administered the Last Rites to a patient in the bed next to Margaret. One of the nurses was abusive to patients and had to be reported to the Sister. When Margaret was eventually discharged, she said that she felt like an escaped convict. Going home was a tremendous emotional experience. 'In our bedroom, the pleasure of being in my own bed was intense'.[2]

Once again, Margaret found that being in her own home helped her to heal, although the 'psychological battle to be "normal" exhausted me'.[3] She found that without both breasts she felt unbalanced, particularly when she walked. There were also decisions to be made about prosthetics. In 1978 there was no reconstructive surgery, as there is today. Margaret was encouraged to have the latest in synthetic

A compulsively readable account

significant sisters

the grassroots of active feminism 1839-1939

margaret forster

breasts. In her memoir, *My Life in Houses*, she describes her excruciating visit to the patient care service that provided them, where she had to restrain herself from running screaming from the room. After the fitting she felt that she had been wrong to give in to pressure. 'Why pretend to have breasts when I no longer had them? . . . Does being a woman mean you have to have breasts?'[4] She began to look at other women and imagine what they would look like without their cleavage. The chemotherapy took nine months to complete. This time no one mentioned the word 'cured' - Margaret was officially only 'in remission'. According to her husband Hunter Davies, Margaret always believed that the cancer would return. For the next thirty years she lived in its shadow and it affected everything she wrote. She began to look more closely at women's lives and their position in society, as well as the mythologies that govern their roles.

In the decade that followed, Margaret Forster wrote four more novels and made two more excursions into the world of non-fiction. *Significant Sisters* is a popular account of eight key figures in the history of the development of feminist ideology, with passages of commentary by the book's author. Written passionately and with great understanding and perception of the difficulties faced by early 'feminists' before a definition of the term had even been coined, Margaret sees them in the context of society as it then was, rather than looking back and judging their words and behaviour by the mores of our own day. In the introduction and conclusion that top and tail the book, Margaret reflects on the influence these women's lives and ideas have had on hers. As a young woman she had wanted 'to have it all', now, as a successful author in her thirties with three children, a husband with a high-flying career and two homes, a cancer survivor, she begins to analyse the cost.

> 'Researching the material for this book,' Margaret admits, 'has . . . radically altered where I stand . . . I have always wanted to be everything - wife, mother, housekeeper, writer. More significant, there was no role I disliked. The problem was not choosing but taking all of them on at the same time and surviving. I have survived, but I do not approve of how I managed it. I think the cost, to myself, has been great.'[5]

Nineteenth-century feminism told women they had to choose between the domestic and the public sphere. Twentieth-century feminism tricked women into believing that they could have both. The ideal of female emancipation - and also its central dilemma - is set out in the quoted words of Elizabeth Cady Stanton: 'The woman is greater than the wife or mother; and in consenting to take upon herself these relations she should never sacrifice one iota of her individuality.'[6] But Margaret Forster understands that the problem for women is much more complex than the authors of seminal feminist texts have been prepared to admit.

'I have gradually come round to understanding that there is still a trap. It isn't marriage itself; it isn't motherhood alone; it is some subtle force which is not yet either fully understood or controlled. There is something in women which prevents them striking out as men do.'[7]

Margaret was also exploring these ideas in her fiction. *Private Papers* (1986), the novel that immediately followed *Significant Sisters*, features a mother who, like Lily Forster, gives up her life for her family in a way that her daughters are unable to accept. Margaret was returning to a subject she had already explored, with devastating clarity, in 1979. *Mother, can you hear me?* (one of her most auto-biographical novels) is an account of mother/daughter relationships and how patterns of relating can be passed down through the generations. The parents are uncannily like Margaret's own. When Angela's father insists 'anyways, I'm managing,' it's the voice of Margaret Forster's father that we hear, and the impossible standards, the unspoken emotional demands of Angela's mother owe much to Lily Forster's selfless devotion and its effect on her daughter. 'She was a Mother, and Mothers stood like rocks, immovable and solid, while all the rest eddied around them. . . A Mother, Angela thought, should be there when you come home to soothe and explain and support.'[8]

It's a standard that Angela finds unattainable, and her failure leaves her full of guilt and self-recrimination. She tries to avoid making her daughter feel the familial obligations that have constricted her own life, creating other problems as she does so. 'It's all much too complicated,' a confused Angela tells her daughter. 'You can't talk glibly about love and duty just like that - I don't know what I feel, except guilty and responsible.'[9]

~~~~~~~~~~~~~~~~~~~

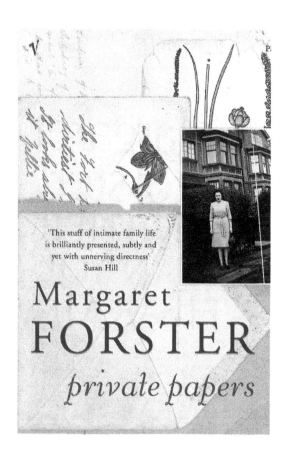

'This stuff of intimate family life
is brilliantly presented, subtly and
yet with unnerving directness'
Susan Hill

Margaret
FORSTER

private papers

8

By now Margaret Forster's own domestic routines were well established. Always an early riser, she got up in the morning and wrote until lunchtime - walking, shopping or doing chores in the afternoons. She lived an almost puritan existence, particularly after the cancer. No tea. One cup of coffee was allowed in mid-morning; she gave up wine, meals were simple with plain food. Margaret went to bed around 9pm.

The morning hours set aside for writing were non-negotiable. As the children grew up and re-located themselves Margaret was able to move into a small room they had built as an extension on top of the bathroom in 1974 to accommodate their growing family. Until 1984, Margaret had written on the living room table - easy for novels, but as she began to write more and more non-fiction, it was necessary to have space for notes and research material. When Hunter gave up his newspaper job to become a freelance writer working from home, it became essential for Margaret to have her own space. She explained in an interview that his methods of working were very different from her own. He made cups of coffee, he wandered round the house, he whistled, he chatted and he was eager to share what he'd just written. Margaret needed seclusion and absolute peace and quiet.

'The minute I walk into this room of my own, I swear I become a different person,' Margaret told the *Guardian*. All her roles as housekeeper, wife and mother disappeared; 'only the writer is left'. Her room had windows on two sides, a bare wooden floor and an old fashioned pedestal desk under the window where she could look out over the gardens at the back of the house. The ground had once been an orchard, divided into sections for each of the houses, but each one still had a fruit tree and in spring she looked down on a sea of blossom. The room was full of light. 'I feel cut off, as though I'm in the sky, suspended and enclosed.' There were books everywhere, on shelves, on the window sills, and piled on the floor. Margaret never used a computer, she wrote by hand on blocks of A4 paper with a fountain pen.

'I believe the whole process of using a pen is part of how I think,' she told the interviewer. 'I'm more careful with the words when changing or erasing them would not be simple. And the handwriting gives me pleasure.'[1] For her editor at Penguin, Alison Samuels, 'Margaret was the perfect author - no-nonsense, feisty, funny, and quick to respond and get on with the job'.[2] Alison lived nearby, so that editing sessions were often held at Margaret's dining table, overlooking the garden. Margaret didn't like editing. She wrote her books quickly from one end to the other without altering anything and preferred not to re-read her work until it was finished. In some of her novels, this lack of editorial rigor is definitely a source of criticism. Hunter Davies would read her work once it was complete and give his opinion. 'I'd always say the same thing: "Not many laughs, petal!" It was always women and relationships'.[3]

Only the winters were spent in London, where they still lived in the Boscastle Road house that she and Hunter had bought when they first married. Margaret firmly resisted moving from it. Summers were always spent in Cumbria, first in a cottage near Caldbeck and then in a larger, more secluded property at Loweswater. As her international reputation grew, Margaret's novels had (as she had herself) remained rooted in Cumbria, although only one is wholly Cumbrian - her gothic romance *The Bride of Lowther Fell*, set in the Caldbeck fells on the very farms where I grew

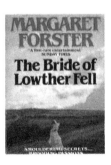

up. But in many of her other novels her characters attend hospitals in Carlisle, or live in a community that is recognisably Cumbrian. If they live in the south, they have working class northern roots which they are trying unsuccessfully to leave behind. While not as self-consciously Cumbrian as those novels written by her contemporary Melvyn Bragg, the influence of Margaret's native landscape on her work is clear.

During the summers at their house in Loweswater, Hunter and Margaret reconnected with family, spent the afternoons walking in the Lakeland fells and often went swimming in the lake. It was a quieter schedule that perhaps suited Margaret better than the more gregarious Hunter, who loved parties and literary 'dos', and would happily, he once admitted 'go to the opening of a fridge!'. Margaret fought, fiercely, to preserve her creative time. Hunter described how he would come home from a walk, or from the pub, to find a sharp note on the mat asking not to be disturbed, or complaining that the phone had been ringing all afternoon - for him!

Success brought all the normal demands made on an established writer - publishers wanted Margaret to publicise her books, literature festivals wanted her to give talks and do workshops - all of which are a drain on a writer's creative energies but which are now part of the standard contract. Although in the late seventies she did consent to be on the BBC's advisory committee on the Social Effects of Television, and to sit on the Arts Council Literature Panel, she steadfastly avoided the literary circus acts that promoting a book now entails. In an interview she explained why;

> 'These days publishers require an awful lot of an author because it's such a cut throat business. The publisher has the author as a

performing animal and they know I can do it because I'm not exactly a shrinking violet but I won't do it. . . I don't do tours, or literary lunches, or book signing sessions I've got that written into my contract. I don't know how public spirited people like Melvyn [Bragg] manage it. I'm a solitary sort of person, and I'm not public spirited so I just stay in the house wherever I am.'[4]

As an adult, Margaret Forster still refused to conform to other people's expectations of what she should do. As well as declining invitations to talk about her books, she was also reluctant to attend the social events and literary networking opportunities her more sociable husband enjoyed. Margaret detested dinner parties. 'I would always rather be somewhere else, preferably at home.'[5] She was one of the celebrities invited to Tony Blair's party at No 10 Downing Street after his election victory. Although she was a committed socialist, Margaret declined.

She was lucky to be well known enough to be able to refuse to do what she found uncomfortable - one of the few authors to maintain her privacy and resist the publicity circuit. It should be a lesson for publishers that her books sell well even without these activities.

She didn't Blog or Tweet either, but Margaret did give interviews and was generous of her time, though she didn't suffer fools gladly. Some journalists found her prickly. One observed that she was 'bossy, easily bored and sharp-tongued'. He taxed her with her abrasive, no-nonsense approach expecting to be rebuffed and was surprised when she was amused; 'When I venture that her aggressive writing style is a pretty accurate reflection of the character behind it she positively delights in confirming the observation. "I hope so! By nature I am aggressive and extremely critical," she laughs, concurring that she will go to her grave arguing the toss with somebody about something or other.'[6]

Margaret always preserved a dignified silence about anything written about her or her work. On the BBC's Desert Island Discs programme, she claimed to relish critical reviews. 'It's as near as you'll ever get,' she remarked, 'to being that fly on the wall and hearing what people really think of you.'[7]

During the eighties and early nineties, Margaret Forster's novels seemed to be more and more concerned with the exploration of sensitive social issues reflecting the novelist's own political sensibility. In *The Battle for Christabel*, the world of politically correct bureaucracy in fostering and adoption is exposed. Christabel is orphaned by her mother's death in a climbing accident. Immediately, there is a battle for who is to have the five year old, since Rowena (a single mother) had not appointed a legal guardian in the event of anything happening to her. Grandmother, aunt, mother's lover, friend and foster mother all have claims. Since Christabel is of mixed race origin, colour and class are an issue and she becomes a victim of the social politics of the day. After a long legal wrangle that benefits no one, Christabel is adopted by strangers. As a reader, you can't feel it's the right decision, but it's a decision and everyone has to live with it. Life is like that.

Mother's Boys (1994) less successfully tackles the modern problem of street crime. It's narrated by two

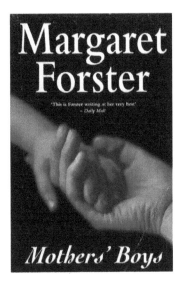

women, the mother and grandmother of two boys involved in a violent, sadistic attack - one as victim, the other as attacker. Together they help each other come to terms with what has happened, and the boys are gradually revealed as much more complex individuals, whose roles are not as clear-cut as they appear at first. Both, it seems, are victims. What the novel lacks is the sense of passionate involvement with the characters and the dense personal detail that informs the books that were to follow. Anita Brookner criticised the novel in the *Spectator*. It was 'very good, but is it art?' It could be a documentary, she observed, 'It could be twenty episodes of Brookside.' Margaret Forster is very clear that it is indeed art. The art of the novel, she believes, 'is about taking the reader into other people's emotions, into their lives and making them, for a while, live that person's life.'[8]

By far the most interesting novel from this period is *Have the Men had Enough?* (short-listed for the *Sunday Express* Book of the Year Award 1989), which was based on Margaret's experience of her mother-in-law's Alzheimer's disease and written, she told an interviewer, out of 'rage and pity'. It is so auto-biographical Margaret referred to it as 'virtually a documentary'.[9] Three female narrators, daughter, daughter-in-law and grand-daughter, cope with Mrs McKay's rapid decline into senility. The men of the family are less involved and the physical and emotional burden of coping falls on the women.

The subtleties of emotional family politics are laid bare with absolute precision, and it's a perceptive study of a family pushed to the limits. For her daughter Bridget, caring for Mrs McKay fulfils a lack in her own life. She gives the love that she wishes had been given to her, hoping, always hoping to get it back, even when her mother is beyond even recognising her. For her daughter-in-law Jenny, Mrs McKay also fills a need, but creates the most immense conflicts, forcing her to decide what is really important, and revalue her own relationships. For grand-daughter Hannah, this is her first real experience of illness, old age and death. Through it she begins to see her mother as a separate individual, and provides a pair of detached eyes through which to see the family

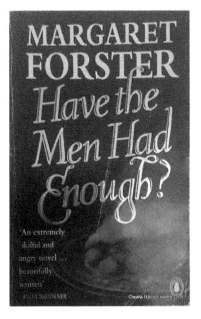

struggle. Her own love for her grandmother, unburdened by the terrible conflicting needs and responsibilities of the adults, remains constant right to the end. It's a moving, satisfying book with moments of high comedy such as the excruciating Sunday lunch when Mrs McKay abandons the cutlery and uses her false teeth as a scoop to get her food from the plate to her mouth.

9

Towards the end of the 1980s, Margaret Forster's work became increasingly weighted towards non-fiction despite Forster's own preference for fiction. Biography, she told an interviewer,

'is a manufactured thing whereas fiction is natural . . . Biography is almost cold blood-ed. I don't mean to say that you don't have enthusiasm for it but the starting point is . . . who would I like to write about, who inter-ests me. Fiction is very quick to me, I rarely spend more than a few weeks on a novel. With biography it's years and years and it splits into very different parts. I mean you've got the research part, going out and looking at sites. If it is modern biography, you've got the going out and meeting people your sub-ject knew. Then there's the sitting down and writing it. So it feels like real work and it's ex-tremely satisfying on that level but it hasn't got what you have to call, the corny word the magic of the novel, this thing that springs up and has its own life. Novels are easy, natural, magic in process and non fiction is very, very hard work and deeply satisfying.'[1]

Fiction, for Margaret, was something easy, that sprung up inside her trying to get out. A novel would take her six or nine weeks, not the years of slog that makes a biography. With fiction, the author is totally in control; with biography the author has always got to be thinking 'Is that true? Is that fair? Is it readable?'[2] Margaret confessed to being unable to work on a novel the way she did on a biography. She said in an interview that she was unable to put a novel away in a drawer for a year and then look at it with all her critical faculties and edit it. 'I probably should, but somehow I can't.' She also confessed to a feeling of loss and sadness when she finished a novel. 'I always start off with tremendous enthusiasm. . . When I finish I do feel sad usually. I can see that I didn't quite pull off what I thought I was going to pull off.'[3]

1988 saw the publication of a biography of Elizabeth Barrett Browning. After the biographical essays of *Significant Sisters*, the narrative experiments of *The Rash Adventurer* and the fictionalised autobiography of *Thackeray*, this was Margaret's first conventional literary biography, weighing in at almost four hundred pages plus notes. Long, detailed biographies were in vogue, and Margaret's was the first full biography of Elizabeth for more than thirty years. In that time, thanks to the tireless digging of a scholar called Philip Kelley, huge amounts of material had emerged shedding light on her early years. He was, Margaret writes, like 'a man obsessed' in his search for lost papers and letters.

Surviving members of the Barrett and Browning families were tracked down and often small hoards of letters, apparently insignificant on their own, filled important gaps in the family story. Diaries which Elizabeth had kept during her adolescence and the years before her marriage, were discovered, and new correspondence emerged between friends and family. Then, in 1983, three volumes of letters between Elizabeth and Miss Mitford were published, giving the public access to one of the poet's most important relationships. Margaret Forster was the first beneficiary of this glut of information. There was now more material available covering Elizabeth's early life than the period of her marriage to Robert Browning - the romantic images could be contextualised and a new, more robust and three dimensional character revealed. It was a gift, Margaret admitted, that would satisfy the 'most greedy' of literary biographers, allowing her to state categorically that; 'No longer is the frail invalid of Wimpole Street a puzzle to us as she waits to hear Robert Browning's step on the stair'.[4]

The emphasis in this biography is on the person rather than the poetry. Elizabeth Barrett Browning's character, her neuroses, her illnesses and the family hothouse that formed her as both woman and writer are skilfully laid before the reader. We know what happened and - most important of all - we know why. The stifling existences imposed on 19th century women with brilliant minds are put before the reader with great clarity. The social restraints that confined them, the brutal untruths they were forced to accept, the battles with biology, make painful reading. In the twenty first century we have almost forgotten how the commands of men, however illogical or irrational or inhumane, were supposed to be obeyed by women without question, male authority backed up by civil and religious law. Probably the best thing about this biography is that it makes Elizabeth's father human, rather than the ogre depicted in some accounts of the poet's life. Given Mr Barrett's character and circumstances, his behaviour becomes understandable, even excusable.

Given that one of the declared aims of the biography was 'to stimulate more interest in Elizabeth Barrett Browning's poetry',[5] it seems strange to find that the book has no quotations or poetic reference other than titles - particularly to *Aurora Leigh*, an important, book-length, poem rich in female politics which charts the growth of a young woman poet just like herself - but the inclusion of literary exposition and quotation would probably have made the book overlong. Margaret Forster solved the issue by publishing a companion volume containing a selection of Elizabeth's poetry with an introduction. The collection spanned her writing life from the age of twenty until she died and showed all aspects of her work as a poet, particularly her feminist, political and religious poetry. All the poems were printed in their original versions as she had prepared them for publication and, wherever possible, in chronological order. We get a glimpse of an author who was passionately political, who believed that poets were obliged 'to tell the real truth' and speak out against injustices and inequalities, particularly the sufferings of women and their inferior social position.

From the beginning, Elizabeth Barrett Browning addressed subjects considered unsuitable for a woman to write about - prostitution, illegitimacy, double standards, the exploitation of women, sexual passion, as well as the more usual territory of motherhood

'She has taken Charlotte's reputation out of lavender for a new generation of admirers'
Independent

VINTAGE
LI*V*ES

Elizabeth Barrett Browning
Margaret Forster

and domesticity. She felt so strongly that women had a duty not to ignore the wrongs done to their sex, she insisted that if women writers did not write about them they had 'better use a pen no more' and 'subside into slavery and concubinage'.[6] Elizabeth was saddened by the lack of role models, writing in a letter to a friend, 'I look everywhere for grandmothers and see none'.[7] Of her contemporaries, she admired only Felicia Hemans and Laetitia Landon.

The selection of poems includes the feminist ballad 'Lady Geraldine's Courtship' and the passionate 'Bianca Among the Nightingales', but omits any of *Aurora Leigh* - her verse novel and arguably Elizabeth's most successful and important poem, tackling the subjects of female education and the double sexual standards of the 19th century. Apparently Elizabeth had abhorred extracts.

Despite this omission, the selection is a good introduction to Elizabeth Barrett Browning's work and includes many of her social reforming poems ('The Cry of the Children', 'A Curse for a Nation', 'Void in Law', 'The Forced Recruit') as well as Part I of *Casa Guidi Windows*, which is an account of the political upheaval in Italy, as witnessed from the windows of the Brownings' apartment, as Italy tried to shake itself free from Austro-Hungarian domination. The *Selected Poems* and Margaret Forster's editorial comments on them are a useful addition to the biography, providing a parallel account of Elizabeth's life and her preoccupations in poetry.

~~~~~~~~~~~~~~~~~~

10

The biography was acclaimed by reviewers. 'Skilful and deeply revealing' wrote the *Sunday Telegraph*. The *Independent* thought that she had scotched 'the myth of the woman poet imprisoned by her father'. 'Margaret Forster has succeeded triumphantly', wrote the *Times*. The biography justly received the Royal Society of Literature Award in 1988. It seems astonishing, given Elizabeth Barrett Browning's status as a literary icon, that Margaret's biography remains today the only comprehensive account of her life. Even more astonishing that it is no longer in print.

Margaret's biographical subjects often have fictional spin-offs. Her award-winning biography of Elizabeth Barrett Browning was soon followed by a novel focussed on the fascinating life story of her maid. It was almost as though she felt that the factual constraints placed on the biographer were too much of a burden and that the story had to be told again in a fictional form. She was not the first person to have done this - fifty years earlier, Virginia Woolf had written a biography of Elizabeth's dog Flush.

Lady's Maid tells the story of Elizabeth Wilson, who gave up her own life and her child, to look after her famous namesake first in England and then in Italy. The novel is able to portray a less sympathetic side of Elizabeth Barrett Browning than the biography - the self-centred mistress whose own interests were paramount and who demanded absolute loyalty at whatever cost to those who served her. Despite an affinity between the two Elizabeths, the class system was rigid and, however intimate the services rendered by Elizabeth Wilson to her namesake, the deeper intimacy of friendship on equal terms could never be attained. As the novel puts it: 'Those who serve can never hope to breach the gap between themselves and those who are served'.[1]

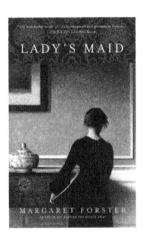

The novel is dedicated to Margaret's friend, the writer and journalist, Valerie Grove - 'another hardworking lass from the north-east'. Margaret didn't have many female friends. She claimed that Hunter was her best friend and her life centred around her family and her writing, leaving little time for anything else. Coffee mornings and girls' nights out were not for Margaret. But she became a confidante for many, giving brusque advice when asked. People told her private things and valued her opinion. Valerie Grove was a writer and a mother and shared some of the nitty-gritty of parenting with Margaret over forty years of neighbourly living. Fay Weldon was another. Valerie tells the story of how the doorbell rang one night and there was Fay on the doorstep, very upset, asking if she could possibly watch the dramatization of her own novel *The Life and Loves of a She-Devil* on Margaret's television as her husband Ron - a jazz musician - wouldn't allow her to watch it on their own set after a row. Margaret, who rarely watched television herself, was happy to oblige.[2]

Daphne du Maurier, an account of the author's life written with the co-operation of her family, was the point where Margaret Forster really came of age as a biographer. The book came about in a way that was almost uncanny. Margaret accidentally knocked against a bookshelf and a book fell to the floor. She picked it up and saw that it was Rebecca, and remembered how much she had loved the book. Margaret wondered if Daphne was still alive and whether anyone had written her biography. The next day she sent a postcard to her publisher Carmen Callil asking whether she would be interested and received a letter back saying 'definitely!' The only problem for Margaret was that Daphne du Maurier was still very much alive and Margaret wasn't willing to tackle the biography of a living person. The following morning she answered the phone and it was the BBC wondering if she would go on air and talk about Daphne who had died the previous evening. Daphne du Maurier's children, when told the story, said that it was their mother picking her biographer from beyond the grave!

Published in 1993, the biography brings the subject vividly to life and grips the reader with a strong narrative. Du Maurier is depicted like a character in one of Margaret's novels - prickly, difficult, at times very badly behaved, but somehow she makes us care about her subject and gives essential insights into her complex, often contradictory personality. Writing the book, Margaret came face to face with both the nightmare and the dream of every biographer, previously undisclosed personal information - in du Maurier's case a lesbian relationship. Margaret Forster had actually finished the book when manuscripts came to light revealing a love affair with Gertrude Lawrence. Not only did she have to begin to rewrite the biography, but there was also the problem of whether the family would allow her to use such controversial material.

In the event Daphne's children were extremely generous about discoveries that were inevitably painful for them, and they courageously stood by their mother and her beliefs about biography. 'She never at any time banned a biography about herself, once she was dead . . . [and believed that] they should try to tell what she called 'all truth'. What she detested were biographies that were 'stereo-typed, dull-asditchwater, or very fulsome praising [sic]'.[3] Another worry was how the British public would react to such revelations about one of their most cherished authors, but the publicity they generated ensured that the book became a best-seller and the controversy soon died down. Margaret said afterwards that she would never forget 'that thrill again of tilling virgin ground, so to speak, and that's why I'll never write another biography'.[4]

Daphne du Maurier was awarded the 1994 Fawcett Book Prize.

In the wake of its success, Margaret appeared on BBC Radio's Desert Island Discs programme, despite not liking music. She admitted in one interview, 'I detest all songs, pop or otherwise. I don't like any music; it is just noise. I prefer total silence.'[5] But the programme was engrossing and her choices gave a fascinating insight into her life.

She chose Benny Goodman playing 'Send in the Clowns' because it brought back memories of her daughter Flora playing the clarinet on summer evenings while she sat in the garden and everyone stopped to listen to the music floating out of the windows. Sydney Bechet's 'Petite Fleur' reminded her of her twenty-first birthday when, at Hunter's instigation, she asked her family for a record player. They also sent record tokens which he happily spent on Beethoven, Sibelius and other music that drove her mad. But he had also chosen jazz and she found she liked that. Bob Marley brought back long trips in the car from London to the Lake District with the children. The Beatles' 'Blackbird Singing in the Dead of Night' reminded her of the time when Hunter brought Ringo Starr back to the house for some home cooking and she discovered too late that he was a vegetarian who didn't like vegetables. Fortunately she had made three puddings, so they had a meal consisting entirely of puddings.

~~~~~~~~~~~~~~~~~~~

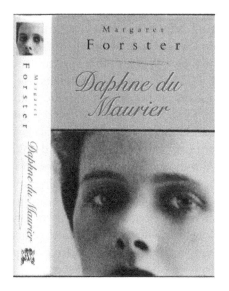

11

Since Daphne du Maurier (in 1993) Margaret Forster seemed to concentrate more and more on non-fiction. In 1997 she wrote (despite her resolution) a biography of the Carr family whose biscuit factory and flour mills dominated her home city of Carlisle. It was called *Rich Desserts and Captain's Thin* and was a fascinating account of one family and the dynasty they created, as well as a beautifully researched piece of local history. Of the novels she published afterwards, several have factional elements. *Isa and May* contains essays on the role of a grandmother in society, *Keeping the World Away* is based partly on the life of Gwen John, and two others - *Shadow Baby* and *The Memory Box* - are rooted in fact and linked to her personal family memoirs *Hidden Lives* and *Precious Lives*. These highly acclaimed autobiographies[1] are possibly Margaret's best books - a beautifully written, sensitive but honest probing of family history and relationships without the disguise of fiction.

Hidden Lives and its sequel were prompted by a suggestion from Margaret's publisher.

'A book called Wild Swans about three generations of Chinese women had done phenomenally well and they were looking for a kind of British version showing whether things had got better for women over the last 100 years. I said I could do my own family but it wouldn't be much of a story because it would all be very ordinary. That's how it began. It wasn't my own idea.'[2]

Before the second half of the twentieth century

working class families rarely merited this kind of written record. Even if they had enough education to be literate, ordinary people didn't keep everyday household letters, had no time or energy left for diaries, often had no money for tombstones and weren't famous enough to be written about by others. In the years before oral history projects became fashionable a whole section of society led 'hidden lives'.

Such anonymity also made it possible for families to keep scandals secret from subsequent generations - and it's a rare family that doesn't have at least one skeleton in the ancestral cupboard. Many of these scandals are the result of the burden of unnatural sexual restraint placed on women for centuries. The birth of a child, which should be an event of human celebration, has - for women not protected by the institution of marriage - been seen as a calamity. Illegitimacy 'ruined' a woman, tainting her own reputation and that of her innocent child, while the father of that child escaped any kind of blame or moral sanction. There is hardly a family in Britain which has not been affected by this harsh moral code during the last two hundred years.

Margaret Forster grew up knowing that there were secrets in her family - questions that went unanswered, subjects avoided. There had been a mysterious visit to her maternal grandmother just before she died by an elderly woman in mourning dress who arrived in a chauffeur-driven car. No one knew who she was and Margaret's grandmother never revealed anything about the purpose of the visit. At her funeral a younger woman came to the door claiming to be her daughter, only to be denied by the rest of the family. It was a mystery, made deeper by the fact that Margaret's grandmother had never talked to any of her children about her life before the age of twenty three - her childhood and adolescence were a blank. As an adult woman in search of her own identity Margaret Forster went to look for the truth. Virginia Woolf famously said that 'women think back through their mothers' and Margaret restates this as: 'We are our past, especially our family past. . . I can't understand my own history unless I understand my grandmother's, my mother's and that of the women like them, the ordinary working-class women from whom I come.'[3]

The result of that search is more gripping and emotionally wrenching than any of Margaret's novels. She found herself retracing the lives of her grandmother and great grandmother.

'It was a strange feeling . . . to be walking past the house where my grandmother worked as a servant. . . The past - my grandmother's, my mother's, my aunts' - did not seem a foreign country to me as I daily walked its streets . . . The empathy with them was so strong, and the recollection of my childhood self so sharp, that we all walked together. But that perhaps is the point of any memoir - to walk with the dead and yet see them with our eyes, from our vantage point.'[4]

In tracing her family history Margaret came face

to face with the centuries old conflict of family versus self that women have always had to deal with and that was also a central issue in her life despite more than a hundred years of feminism and social reform. The quality of life at the end of the twentieth century is undoubtedly much improved - 'everything, for a woman, is better now, even if it is still not as good as it could be.' But there is still the primitive pull of biology, love and duty that is particular to women and will probably always have to be negotiated by those who - like Margaret Forster - decide that they want to have it all.

~~~~~~~~~~~~~~~~~~~

12

Shadow Baby - the novel that followed - is based on Margaret's grandmother's story, beautifully imagined. Two illegitimate girls born seventy years apart, go in search of their histories and it's not until the

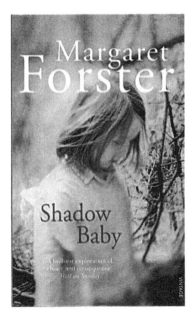

end of the book that the connection between the two births is revealed. The novel is a frank exploration of the respective values of the times they lived in and their effect on women's lives - one cannot help but conclude that it was not so much the illegitimacy that threatened the stability of the family unit, but the lengths people had to go to to hide it. Motherhood is also closely examined in the different relationships the children have with their adoptive and birth parents. Much of personal identity is to do with reflected likenesses - knowing who you are is, in part, knowing who you take after. This essential factor is missing in an adopted family, however strong the emotional bond between individuals. Margaret spells out the consequences of this very clearly.

The Memory Box, one of her most popular novels, continues to explore this subject. It is informed by Margaret's experience with cancer - of being told at thirty-six with three young children, that she had a serious, life-threatening illness. In the novel, the heroine, Catherine, has been orphaned as a baby and brought up by a stepmother. Fiercely loyal to the person she regards as her mother, she has consistently refused to think of her birth mother at all, or to open the box left by the dying Susannah for her tiny daughter. Only at the age of thirty-one - the same age her mother had been when she died - does Catherine open the box and begin to solve the riddle of its contents and her mother's identity, discovering at the same time a great deal about her own. 'In the slippery world of family secrets, Catherine learns that her mother is not the only woman with a hidden past. She has to confront her own repressed memories, and admit what she has always refused to acknowledge: Susannah's genetic influence.' *The Memory Box*, writes a reviewer, 'tantalisingly explores the consequences, sometimes affecting several generations, of suppressing or massaging vital information.'[1]

But Margaret Forster had reservations about the novel, which she expressed in some of her interviews. She had second thoughts about what she had included in the Memory Box itself; 'I do feel that I probably didn't quite get the right articles in the box. I tried very hard but I think some of them were a mistake, such as the pictures, and irritating to the reader.'[2] She also had concerns about the ending, as well as the overall structure, confessing in an interview she did for Penguin

'. . . it wasn't really as successful as I would have

liked it to have been. I mean, I say that at the end of every book but I particularly felt it with this one. I thought maybe I had made Catherine too angry and not sympathetic enough and because I wanted it to be real and feel real there had to be lots of loose ends. I have had letters complaining about the loose ends and I had to write back and say Yes, but I was trying to make it real and in real life you don't know what happened, you can't fill in the gaps.'[3]

Shadow Baby was published in 1996, in the same year that Margaret's eldest daughter Caitlin Davies published her first novel, *Jamestown Blues*. Caitlin had been writing since she was a child, but despite having parents who were successful authors, getting into print hadn't been easy. 'I finished my first complete novel at 19, and despite my parents being writers, I had no idea what to do with it, so I made a pile of books I'd enjoyed reading, and sent it off to a handful of publishers. Surprise! They all sent it straight back. So then I wrote another novel. And another.'[4] Eventually Caitlin found an agent who placed *Jamestown Blues* with Penguin.

Caitlin was currently married and living in Botswana, where she worked first as a teacher and then as a journalist in a rural community. Caitlin 'was posted to Maun, a remote up country settlement of deep sand tracks, magnificent lightning storms and swampy waterways where hippos splashed.'[5] It was as far from London life as it was possible to be and Caitlin fell in love with the country and its people.

She and her husband lived very simply in a traditional house and Caitlin tried to integrate herself into his extended Botswana family. A second book, this time historical, *The Return of El Negro*, was published two years later by a South African publisher and it was the beginning of a career in writing for another family member, achieved purely on her own merits. Few readers are aware that Caitlin is the daughter of Margaret Forster and Hunter Davies - the family connections are never invoked and privacy is zealously preserved.

~~~~~~~~~~~~~~~~~~~~

MARGARET

PRECIOUS LIVES

FORSTER

BY THE AUTHOR OF *HIDDEN LIVES*

'Margaret Forster's books hold you in their grip and linger in the mind...
Precious Lives is unputdownable' MARY WESLEY, *EXPRESS*

13

In the second part of her family memoir, *Precious Lives*, Margaret Forster examines how individuals deal with approaching death and how knowledge of its imminence affects their families, by telling two very different stories - her sister-in-law Marion's premature and brutally quick decline from cancer, and her father's more gradual disengagement at the end of a longer than average life. Margaret never shirks an honest examination of her own motives and emotions. She watches the apprehension of Marion's visitors, 'Visiting the dying is so very tricky . . . There's not a single book of etiquette on how to be polite and say the right thing.'[2] The knowledge that Marion may only have a few months to live also affected what had been a close relationship with Margaret, who now found herself on the other side of an invisible barrier.

> 'I sat directly opposite her while she tried to sip the wretched soup. Too hot? Too thick? Queries about soup, and she was dying. It was ridiculous. . . But . . What did I so badly want to say that she didn't already know? That I was sorry she was dying? . . . Sorry, indeed. That I was sad, upset, distraught, furious? All about my feelings, and who wanted to know

those? They were obvious, and irrelevant. I went on sitting there, while she went on slowly, slowly spooning soup into herself.'[3]

Margaret also finds herself amazed - and at times enraged - at her father's fatalistic stoicism in the face of increasing disability and the loss of dignity and quality of life. 'In my father's opinion it was not up to you to pre-empt fate. When your number was up, it was up - that sort of homespun philosophy.' What she observes in the case of her sister-in-law and her father is that 'the moment people actually were dying the struggle to hold on to life became compulsive and fierce.'[4]

The relationship between Margaret Forster and her father had never been close, but as their roles became reversed by his increasing ill health, Margaret fulfilled what she saw as her duty towards him, despite chafing at the burden of it. She constantly questioned her own need to do this.

'Duty sounds such an ugly, cold, hard word, signifying a lack of love or pleasure or tenderness . . . It was awful to be going to visit my father out of duty. I wanted to be going to see him out of anything but that. I wanted to discover within myself feelings of genuine warmth and love, but I couldn't.'[5]

Even as she analysed her feelings and labelled them, Margaret was aware of something else - something much more complicated. A bond created by family relationship often repeated in the old proverb that blood is thicker than water. 'There was something there . . . which was either not quite duty or which softened it into a feeling less repugnant.' Something that compelled her to telephone him every day, write weekly letters and endure painful visits during the five months she lived in Cumbria. And Margaret finally acknowledged that, though her duty was informed by gratitude and pity, there was still something else.

> 'Even if feeling better about being motivated by duty and gratitude and compassion . . . cheered me up, there was still a piece missing from the puzzle when I tried to understand the power my father had over me . . . What I was seeing, in these years of my father's final decline, was evidence of some inner power to which it was impossible not to respond.'[1]

What she had not added into the equation was her father's indomitable personality, against which she had battled as a child, but which now grudgingly excited admiration.

When he died at the age of ninety-six Margaret Forster felt, not the great relief she had always expected to feel when his death eventually happened, but shock, and regret that she had not been there with him. Looking at his body in the funeral chapel afterwards, she was surprised to feel 'a certain tenderness and sadness' for a man that she had actively hated as a child, though he had given her little cause.

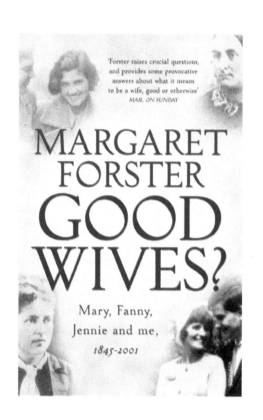

'Forster raises crucial questions, and provides some provocative answers about what it means to be a wife, good or otherwise'
MAIL ON SUNDAY

MARGARET
FORSTER
GOOD
WIVES?

Mary, Fanny,
Jennie and me,
1845-2001

14

The honesty of self analysis that makes these two memoirs such compulsive reading is also the quality that informs another of her non-fiction titles, *Good Wives*. Over the decades the social status of 'the wife' has altered, and with it the way we use the words. As Margaret Forster remarked in an interview: 'Once upon a time to say someone was a good wife was the highest compliment you could pay. Today, if you say someone is a good wife it's the biggest insult you can offer. You are inferring that she is nothing else'.[1]

Returning to the themes of women's role in society explored earlier in *Significant Sisters*, Margaret tells the story of three very different wives - Mary Livingstone, Fanny Stevenson and Jennie Lee. It is not just an account of their lives, but also of hers; not just a biography, but an account of the difficulties and dilemmas of practical feminism in the twentieth century. Margaret Forster describes her own experience of marriage and her struggles with practical feminism as a wife and mother.

She acknowledges the difficulties posed by hardline feminist ideology, which never seemed to take account of the fact that women might actually desire children and wish to nurture them; that they had nesting instincts that might be satisfied by menial domestic tasks; that they loved and desired other human beings whose needs had equal priority with their own; that the much-vaunted right to a career for women might (as with their male counterparts) amount to nothing more than serving in a shop or drudging in a factory - an economic transaction that brought little fulfilment except for the money it provided. Margaret takes a long hard look at four different approaches to these female dilemmas, and asks, 'Why, in the twenty-first century, in a social climate where it is acceptable to live in a partnership, and even to have children within one without any stigma, why . . . does any woman still want to be a wife?'[2]

The book is subtitled 'Mary, Fanny, Jennie and me' and each biography is followed by a section of autobiographical comparison and analysis where Margaret Forster lays bare the history of her own ambivalent relationship with marriage. 'I never wanted to be a wife,' she declares, 'That feeble creature who obeyed.' But in the end she too capitulated, surprised that, though it was no longer necessary for a woman to marry in order to be with a man or to have children, she still wanted to do it. Feeling guilty that she was compromising her principles, she insisted that she was getting married on her own terms, to avoid causing grief to her parents. She wore an antique silver ring rather than a conventional gold band and squirmed every time she was referred to as 'Mrs Davies', but is prepared to admit with the grace of hindsight that there was a certain unacknowledged pride in the 'that title and the badge of office'.

In researching the book Margaret was shocked to

find that 'once the personal details of each woman's day-to-day existence are revealed', despite the time lapse between Mary Livingstone, Fanny Stevenson, Jennie Lee and herself, 'how similar their difficulties were to my own during forty years of being a wife'.[3] It's a statement most women would agree with, despite the fact that 'a wife today is not, or need not be, the same creature' as a wife fifty or a hundred and fifty years ago. But the personal adjustments that have to be made are the same then as now - the struggle for space, the compromises, the loss of minor freedoms - whether married or simply living together. What has not changed is the basic nature of human beings, men and women and their individual and collective needs.

Margaret Forster reveals a great deal about her own personality in this book - particularly how much she values independence. 'A good wife is very definitely an independent wife, one who does not rely entirely on her husband for sustenance of every kind.' Many would not agree with this statement - there are relationships which last and thrive because one party is a giver and the other a taker and they fulfil each others' needs perfectly. But for Margaret 'independence has been of such vital importance to me that I've perhaps made it into a rod with which to beat my back.'[4] She has refused to enter into the nurturing wife-as-nurse, or wife-as-mother roles so many women fall into. Men should be encouraged to look after themselves. 'I think wives should be tough. They should refuse to become surrogate mothers.'

When asked by a newspaper about the success

of her own long marriage, Margaret replied that it was mainly 'a matter of luck. We met. We married, We've always got along. But I certainly don't have any magic formula'. Her approach was controversial; 'I'm always amazed when I read about couples having "struggled through" to reach their Golden Wedding anniversary, or whatever. It seems to me that if you have to "fight", or "struggle" or "work" to save your marriage, it's not worth saving.'[5] Margaret and Hunter were polar opposites. He loved parties and social contact, was a regular, founder, member of the Groucho Club, and an active football supporter. Margaret was reclusive and hated sport. Hunter liked a bit of glamour; Margaret never wore make-up and dressed very plainly. They rarely went out together socially and she never read his books, though he usually read hers. Joint tasks were divided on traditional lines; Hunter managed the money and the garden and Margaret did the housework and the cooking. Acquaintances were mystified by the longevity of their marriage.

Of much more difficulty than achieving a good relationship with her husband was the problem of reconciling the conflicting demands of motherhood and wifehood. 'Being a good mother seems to me so much harder than being a good wife. . . I had what would be termed "separation difficulties", having confidence only in my own caring.' Margaret found it difficult to leave her children with anyone else, a baby-sitter or a relative, even if that meant not being able to accompany her husband to functions or on trips abroad 'I put what I thought of as the best interests of my children before his pleasure. And he didn't like it.'

One incident, recorded as fact in *Good Wives*[**6] and as fiction in *Mother, can you hear me?*,[7] reveals how Margaret was persuaded to leave the children with a retired nurse who lived nearby and had often offered to babysit while she and Hunter went to the cinema. Her worst fears were realised when the manager walked down the aisles asking if there was a Mr and Mrs Davies in the house? The baby had begun screaming and 'Nursey' had been unable to calm him. This reinforced Margaret's conviction that her children could not safely be left with anyone else, though she admits now that her over-protectiveness towards her children was perhaps unjustified - 'It sounds so ridiculous now.'[8] But almost every mother will understand her dilemma.

The demands made on the 'public' wife are also addressed in the book. Margaret Forster is very critical of Hillary Clinton and Mary Archer, who, she asserts, made a big mistake by appearing to condone their husbands' behaviour. 'All one can hope is that in private these public wives speak their minds. If they don't, then they are failing their husbands as much as their husbands have failed them.'[9]

What is most interesting in *Good Wives*, particularly to me as a writer and a woman, is how Margaret dealt with the conflicting importance of 'his work' and 'her work'. From the beginning of their marriage Margaret was not only a writer, but a writer whose work was publicly valued, yet she admits that - probably on the grounds of relative financial status - it was

Hunter's job that was the 'real' job, hers the one that could be put aside. 'It seemed entirely proper that when things were tough my work should go on hold and that he should be protected from whatever circumstances were making them tough.' Even when Hunter left full-time journalism to become a freelance author the situation remained the same.

> '"I have to go and work now," he was given to announcing loudly at crucial moments. Somehow I never said it. Partly this was because writing had never seemed as important to me as the children, but also - and this was irrational - it was because I couldn't rid myself of the belief that what he was doing was more serious.' [10]

This admission saddens, but does not surprise. There is, ingrained in women's psyche, even in the most successful of us, a natural inclination to put others' needs before our own and to undervalue our own achievements. Margaret, the author - at that point - of more than twenty books, many of them best-sellers, admitted that, had she ever been forced to choose between her family and herself, her family would have come before her work. 'I am not proud of this. It is not right or rational. . . I am profoundly grateful that my sort of work has never demanded a straight choice from me.'[11] As a child Margaret saw her own mother having to make that choice and swore she would never do the same, but as an adult woman in the face of the emotional realities of a relationship, realised that she would have done exactly what her mother had done if it had ever been demanded.

~~~~~~~~~~~~~~~~~~~~

15

By 2002, after almost forty years of writing, Margaret's pen had never been sharper or more prolific. She was without a doubt one of English literature's most consistently high-achieving practitioners. But, though reader response was full of praise - an appreciation that was reflected in her sales - major awards and literary recognition had been slow to come. People speculated that it was Margaret's self-imposed seclusion that had denied her inclusion in those literary award lists. Or possibly she had been a victim of the 'literary establishmentarianism' that decides who is in or out of the magic circle, where youth and 'marketability' are valued, a world in which the word 'readable' is still a critical term.

Between 2002 and 2015, Margaret Forster published some of her most accomplished work. Her instinctive handling of a narrative and her fascination with other people's lives come together to produce a reliably good read - from the first page you know you are in safe hands and can sail gently away on a fictional voyage without fear of shipwreck.

In 2003 Margaret produced *Diary of an Ordinary Woman*, 1914-1995. It uses a narrative device beloved of 19th century authors purporting to be a real diary of a real person, discovered and 'edited' by the author in the same way that *Jane Eyre* was originally published as 'the Autobiography of a governess edited by Currer Bell'. [It also echoes Margaret's 'autobiography' of Thackeray]. The fiction is so beautifully crafted that it's difficult to believe that the whole is a novel rather than an autobiography. The cover even has photographs, shopping lists, ration books and scraps of handwritten letters, as if this is a memoir or a biography. Margaret brings all her skills as a novelist, memoirist and biographer together to create the illusion.

Millicent King is the archetypal 'ordinary' woman of the 20th century, whose life has been scarred by two world wars, economic and social upheaval. When Millicent was born in 1901, there were no movies, no motor cars, no aeroplanes, you looked at the moon through a telescope, Mars had little green men on it, Queen Victoria was still alive, women didn't have the vote and were definitely second class citizens. In the absence of the welfare state people starved, went barefoot and died of minor ailments. It was every man and woman for themselves, with crossed fingers, a quick tap on wood and a shudder in the direction of Fate. By the time Millicent died in 1999 the universe had turned on its head. The book jacket bills her as an 'ordinary woman' living through 'extraordinary times'.

Margaret Forster skilfully sets up the illusion of edited autobiography in her introduction, which gives an account of how she 'found' the story;

'In May 1999 I received a letter from a stranger, Joanna King.... Joanna had read a memoir I'd written (*Hidden Lives*, about my grandmother and mother) and, because it was the story of two ordinary women with no claim to fame, it had made her wonder if I might agree that there was some value in Millicent King's diaries as a social document.'[1]

In an interview Margaret revealed that the book began with the discovery of real diaries recording a life from 1914 to 1995. 'I got a letter from the person to whom it's dedicated, saying that her mother was 98 and she'd kept a diary since she was 13.' Margaret's account of how she 'found' Millicent King's diaries was based on fact. 'Up to the point where I go to see the lady that's exactly how it happened, but then the woman's granddaughter got very upset and said that her grandmother had promised her the diaries . . .'[2] The real documents were tantalisingly off-limits. Margaret decided to continue, but with fictional diaries and a fictional main character, though the concept would be the same.

The novel becomes meta-fiction, as Margaret's editorial process, both as fictional and actual editor, is recorded. After reading the diaries and being intrigued and captivated by them, the 'I' of the introduction realises that:

'Editing would involve a rigorous selective process which, because it would be done according to my particular tastes, might not please Millicent. There would

110

also have to be a certain amount of bridging work and to do it I'd have to research all kinds of background material . . . But I had no doubts at all that I wanted to do it, to 'make something', if I could of an ordinary woman's life, so meticulously recorded.'[3]

In an interview Margaret admitted that 'Ordinariness does fascinate me . . . It fascinates a lot of people. You're going on a train and you're passing all those dreary backyards, mile after mile, and you

Is There Anything You Want?

a novel

Margaret
FORSTER

can't help looking at them and thinking, "what lives, what's going on there?"'[4] But the novel's introduction ends with a question; 'I now wonder if there is any such thing as an ordinary life at all.'[5]

It's an interesting narrative structure; the 'editor's' comments and bridging paragraphs provide an alternative point of view and a contrasting 'voice' to Millicent King's diary entries and enable gaps in the story to be filled in. The device was so successful that many readers (and some booksellers) thought that the book was non-fiction, despite the careful statement on the corner of the book jacket, under the title, that it was 'A Novel'. Public reaction was very positive. Helen Falconer in the *Guardian* wrote that '*Diary of an Ordinary Woman* is not simply a traditional "novel in diary form", but more like *the incredibly detailed forgery of an unlived life.*'[6] The italics are mine, because it seems the perfect definition of what a novel aims to be.

~~~~~~~~~~~~~~~~~~~

16

There's hardly a blip between *Diary of an Ordinary Woman* published in 2003 and Margaret's next novel, *Is There Anything You Want?*, in 2005. But during the period when this book was being conceived and written, Margaret had once again to put her family first when her daughter Caitlin arrived back in London from Botswana in December 2002 with a small child. The traumatic events which led to her departure are told in Caitlin's moving memoir called *A Place of Reeds*, published in 2005. 'Maum was my home,' she wrote, 'and I never thought I'd leave.' She had gradually discovered that the country she loved had a darker face - a growing drugs trade and one of the highest HIV rates in the world. Domestic violence was commonplace and there was little respect for women. 'I estimated that a woman was raped in Botswana every 12 minutes'.[1] Given that Aids was so prevalent, being raped could be a death sentence for the woman.

When Caitlin became involved in a group that provided counselling and help for victims of rape, she herself became a target. After a particularly violent incident, she reluctantly made the decision to leave. Caitlin found it hard to settle back in England and her small daughter found it even harder. They were traumatised by violent events, cold, homesick, and worried about the future. For the first few months Caitlin lived at her parents' house, in the room that had been hers as a child. She found a nursery for her daughter, went back into teaching and was able to find a home for them both in North London. The house she moved into became the centre of a plot for a new novel *The Ghost of Lily Painter*.

In 2004 Margaret delivered *Is there Anything you Want?* to her agent and it was published in January 2005 by Chatto and Windus. It is one of Margaret's most absorbing novels and tells the story of a group of very different women whose lives glance against each other in the breast cancer clinic of St Mary's Hospital. As the novel describes them 'all these women were in travail, between health and sickness, hope and despair'.[2] They all live in a northern town very like Carlisle, though it is never named, and the descriptions of the run-down hospital, due for demolition, will echo in the memories of any readers who visited the old Cumberland Infirmary. The peeling cream paint, the drooping ceiling tiles, the makeshift partitions of the clinics, the dreary corridors, are all perfectly evoked. They are the setting for displays of fear, anger, false courage and denial - all the emotions experienced by patients and staff.

Chrissie is a young doctor who can no longer cope with the daily pressure of overcrowded clinics and the necessity of delivering life-shattering news to the women she sees. Edwina, a patient who is years in remission, still can't believe she will live and struggles with depression. Ida is working class, overweight, unhappily married and has panic attacks. Rachel, a solicitor, covers her fears with a veneer of professional calm, though privately she can barely hold her life together. But the most impressive character in the whole book, complex and intricately drawn, is Mrs Hibbert - the bossy upper-class woman nobody likes, who is a hospital Friend, forcing her assistance on anyone who seems to need it. She is overbearing, outrageous, utterly controlling, but also vulnerable, courageous and capable of profound perception and kindness at the most unexpected moments.

It was one of the novels that provoked an editorial argument with her publisher. Margaret's editor felt that it was too bleak. Margaret sent Alison one of her famous postcards, saying, 'If you were Charlotte Brontë's editor, you'd have tried to make her put jokes into Jane Eyre!'[3] But she was eventually persuaded to lighten one of the characters and introduce more humour into the book.

The novel was well reviewed. *The Guardian* commented that 'there can be few other contemporary authors who have evoked middle England with greater accuracy. . . Roots are Forster's forté. Her characters are not mere products of their time and place but they are under constant, cruel pressure to act as if they are'. The reviewer contrasted Margaret's work with Anita Brookner whose novels tend to go over the same territory again and again. With Margaret, 'no two stories are the same, and each new permutation offers insights never signalled in its predecessors'.[4]

The reaction of general readers was mixed; for some the book was too raw - one, a nurse who worked in a cancer clinic, was disturbed that the book seemed to offer so little optimism and failed to show how cancer patients often supported each other. 'I kept hoping that one of Forster's character would find this strength and reach out to the others, but all her characters were isolated and lonely.'[5] Others found it refreshing to find what is often a taboo subject written about with such frankness. Few knew that the novel was rooted in Margaret Forster's experience of her own brush with cancer, now securely in the past. She had been discharged by the consultant after ten years and was no longer required to go for check-ups.

~~~~~~~~~~~~~~~~~~~~

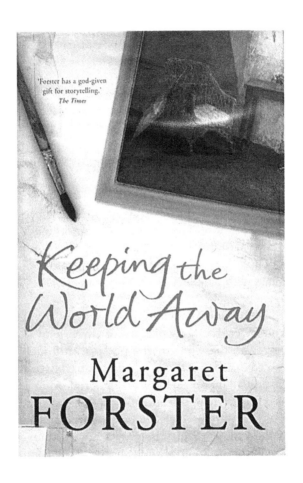

'Forster has a god-given
gift for storytelling.'
The Times

Keeping the World Away

Margaret
FORSTER

17

In 2006 Margaret published *Keeping the World Away*. Again this is the blend of fact and fiction that Margaret does to perfection. Gwen John's famous diary entry is used as an epigraph and almost feels like the author's own manifesto;

> 'Rules to keep the world away; Do not listen to people (more than is necessary); Do not look at people (ditto); Have as little intercourse with people as possible; When you come into contact with people, talk as little as possible . . .'

It is the story of a painting - the first of a series of beautiful, enigmatic depictions of Gwen John's own room - and the women who possess it through the troubled decades of the twentieth century, two world wars and all the social upheaval that followed. It begins with Gwen herself and her childhood struggle to oppose her parents' expectations and study art alongside her brother Augustus. Eventually she moves to Paris, becomes Rodin's lover and paints a picture of her room which is then given to her friend Ursula who packs it in a valise and loses it on the way back to England. Ursula knows that she has lost something important. 'It contains a treasure,' Gwen had told her, but Ursula had never had time to find out what it was.

Gwen has painted into the canvas a truth she has learned painfully over the turbulent years of her attempts to escape her family and learn to paint, and her desperate affair with Rodin, knowing that her passion and need far outstripped his. As he wanted her less and less, she realised that she had to learn to survive on her own. The small painting of a corner of her room, without anyone in it, was painted in rage and frustrated desire. It is a symbol of what she knows she must learn - it's an image of contentment, a life fulfilled, 'well satisfied', though Gwen is still anything but. 'It was a cheat. It was full of hope, yet she was losing hope.'

Ursula's valise goes to a lost property office in London, where it's mistakenly brought home by a young man searching for his wife's valise mislaid while on honeymoon in Paris. His wife's sister, Charlotte, 'clever and peculiar', discovers the painting and, after waiting for three months for the painting to be claimed, is finally able to possess it for a brief period before her parent's house is burgled and the painting stolen. What it teaches Charlotte is that she hasn't enough talent to be the artist she had wanted to be and that she must pursue a different career.

The novel is intricately plotted. Charlotte meets a much older Ursula in a chance encounter in Paris, unaware of the connection between them and there are brief, tenuous links of relationship with the subsequent owners, all oblivious to the one thing they have in common. The stolen painting is bought from

119

a market stall after the First World War by a wounded veteran who had once been in love with Charlotte. He gives it to the woman he now lives with, Stella, who sells it to an artist in order to get enough money to leave him because his possessive need for her is stifling her own talents. Stella escapes to make her own life somewhere else.

This is the message that the painting conceals. It is a message about the enfranchisement of women through art. For Lucasta, Ailsa and Madame Verlon, who all briefly possess the canvas, and for Gillian who eventually inherits it, the message is the same: Live your own creative life - don't be pressured by others, by family, or by love, to be anything but wholly yourself. There is no hint that this can be done in the company of others; isolation and seclusion are essential. 'The artist . . . had painted it to keep the world away,' the book ends, 'If it helped others to do the same, her purpose was fulfilled.'

Described by one reviewer as 'A fine novel . . . an inspired reflection on the redemptive potential of art,'[1] it was popular with readers who had not previously been fans of Margaret's novels. Words like 'unputdownable' were used. It also sold in America, the first book to appeal to US readers for more than a decade. The *New York Times* liked her 'writing style, which is evocative without being ornate' and commented that 'Gwen John's reputation has grown recently, and so should Margaret Forster's'.[2] Elsewhere readers and reviewers on the - increasingly important - blogosphere, liked the questions the novel asked;

'What makes art art? Why are the lives of starving artists . . . seen as glamorous and therefore paths that should be envied? What makes a work of art meaningful? Does meaning stem from the artist's intention or what the beholder takes away from it? Can an artist live a well balanced life (practice monogamy, raise a family, have other interests) or must he/she devote his/her complete self to his/her art? While each of the characters attempts to answer these questions, they stumble often, proving that there is no right or wrong answer, which is what makes art - and its creation - so alluring and the book a worthwhile read.'[3]

Keeping the World Away is likely to be one of Margaret Forster's classic novels, written during a period when she was working at her fastest and best. It also led to Margaret being asked to write an essay to introduce the National Portrait Gallery's portrait awards for 2006. The resulting publication is a very interesting glance at portraits and biography. In it, Margaret confesses that she has had, for two years, a copy of Gwen John's self-portrait propped up on her desk, 'so that if I lift my eyes even for a minute from what I'm writing, Gwen John looks back at me.' It was, Margaret wrote, an essential part of getting to know one's subject. 'Every biographer needs a portrait of their subject before they can even begin to think of how to delineate a life'. After researching the painter's life and character for the novel, Margaret realised that she was beginning to read other things into the self 'as presented by the painter'.[4]

In the essay, Margaret explores the history of portraiture, how symbols of wealth and status were more important in the painting than a likeness of the subject. She comments on how few women there are in the public gallery 'only queens and aristocratic ladies made the grade.' It was a long time before women 'began to appear because of their achievement rather than their status' and real character began to appear in their faces. Suddenly 'there are layers of meaning to decipher and . . . it is the women who benefit most'. She focuses on a self-portrait of Mary Beale, painted in 1665 - a professional artist whose 'portrait is a biography in itself'.

It is the narratives in the portraits that interest Margaret rather than painterly technique, and it is the narratives of women's lives that draw her in - the novelist's fascination with character and relationship. On the portrait of Nobel prize-winning chemist *Dorothy Hodgkin* by Maggi Hambling, Margaret comments that 'all her life is there, or rather what mattered most, the work strewn about her. I wonder, looking at it, whether there was any conversation at all, or was the artist ignored?'

Laura Knight's self-portrait, standing in front of her nude model, contrasting strongly with her own clothed form, also comes in for discussion. 'The relationship between artist and model, between woman and woman is intriguing . . . why the colour red? . . . And why the cardigan, worn as it is with that stylish hat? . . . does it matter? . . . The need to know exactly

what was going on that day in the studio is so strong.
It's enough to make a biographer desperate.' [5]

~~~~~~~~~~~~~~~~~~~~

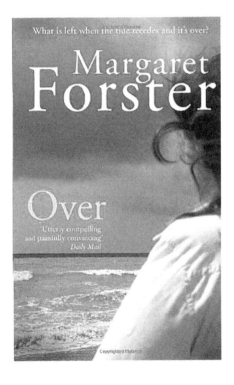

18

In the same year, 2006, Margaret published what many believe to be her finest novel and it was, fittingly, short-listed for the Orange Prize. It had been called 'Afterwards', but Karen Seiffert beat Margaret to the publication post with the same title and the book was re-named *Over*, both titles taken from a quote in the novel when the character thinks: 'It is Over. It's been over for two years. It is Afterwards that matters - now'.[1]

Over is one of Margaret Forster's shortest books, coming in at just two hundred pages, and it's written in the first person, not a point of view that she uses often. The novel is about what the death of a child does to a family. Eighteen year old Miranda has drowned in a sailing accident. Her mother Louise, the narrator, believes that she has coped better with grief than her husband Don, who is determined that someone must be to blame for the accident, someone must pay. Louise remarks that 'the thought of actually recovering is something I think he cannot bear. To recover would, for him, be the greatest betrayal of all.'[2] Neither parent takes on board the terrible effect of the tragedy on Miranda's siblings, who not only have to cope with their own loss, but their parents' grief and the destruction of their previously secure family framework.

While she was writing, Margaret had in her mind the campaigns waged by two men in particular whose daughters had died in tragic events. John Ward, whose daughter Julie had been murdered in Kenya, and Dr Jim Swire who lost his daughter in the Pan Am disaster at Lockerbie. Both men have fought to find the truth. 'It does seem to me that there's something in men, an anger that drives them on. Whereas I think women tend to feel that they must "move on" . . . If only for the sake of our other children we have to try to be happy again.' [3]

Over received stunning reviews, and was among the twenty books long-listed for the 2007 Orange prize for fiction. It was a very strong list which also included the book which had pre-empted Margaret's original title, *Afterwards* by Rachel Seiffert. There were other big award winners competing for the prize; Stef Penney's *The Tenderness of Wolves*, *Half of a Yellow Sun* by Chimamanda Ngozi Adichie, and Kiran Desai's *The Inheritance of Loss*. Margaret's novel didn't make the shortlist, but it produced a huge response from readers. 'I usually get a trickle of letters about my novels, but this one has produced a deluge' - many of them from parents or relatives of people who had lost their children. Margaret hoped that the book might help bereaved parents 'in however small a way'.[4]

Publishers usually hope for another book almost immediately to capitalise on the success of an award with all the extra publicity it generates, but Margaret's next novel took longer to write and there were also delays in the editing process that meant a three year gap between books. *Isa and May* was published in 2009 and is another blend of fact and fiction.

Isa (short for Isabel) and May (short for Margaret) are the narrator's grandmothers. They are as different as chalk and cheese, Isa is upper class, May is working class; they have very different personalities and have never got on with each other. There is an 'animal-like antipathy' between them. The first-person narrator, Issy, is obsessed by them 'or, more precisely, I am obsessed by their significance, without being sure what that is'. This has almost been wished on her by her parents, who christened her Isamay after them both because she was delivered by her grandmothers, arriving quite by accident on the bathroom floor before the ambulance could arrive. Issy is Isa's only grandchild, for May the only female grandchild and so she is special to both.

Perhaps for this reason, Issy is doing an MA in Women's Studies on the subject of grandmothers and their importance in society. Her dissertation covers historical figures such as Elizabeth Fry, Queen Victoria, George Sand and Edith Millais and we follow Issy's research into their roles. Issy has a very difficult relationship with her demanding supervisor Claudia who questions her assumptions and subjects her conclusions to rigorous analysis. Issy has trouble with her parents too - both high achievers with high expectations for their daughter. But at twenty-eight Issy still has no 'sense of direction' and recognises their disappointment in her. She is living with a man called Ian she met in an airport, who won't talk to her about his family relationships at all and quite definitely doesn't want to make a new family with Issy, however much he cares for her. So, when she discovers she's pregnant and finds herself strangely reluctant to have a termination, things get very tricky.

Issy's research soon extends to her own family and there too she finds that things aren't as simple as she had thought. There are secrets and silences. It's a rare family that isn't touched by illegitimacy. Issy finds that she feels more comfortable with the past than with the present 'the past is so secure', the present uncomfortable, the future a worry. Issy is in no hurry to confront the future, but when her child is born, that's just what she has to do.

There's a great deal of historical detail in the novel. As Issy researches her subjects and writes up her dissertation, the novel becomes a meditation on the role of grandmothers in society and within the family. It asks a lot of questions; 'is grandmothering . . . all about second chances? Or about repetition?' What is the role of genetics? Is an adoptive grandmother as good as the real thing?

Although published reviews were welcoming, the reader response was less positive. Even ardent fans of Margaret's work felt that the novel lacked some essential quality. Where other novels attracted four and five star reviews on Amazon, *Isa and May* only managed to average three. Some readers felt that the book might have been more successful as non-fiction - a straightforward look at the grandmothers that Issy was researching, perhaps blended with some of Margaret's own experiences as a grandmother, along the lines of *Good Wives* where she contributed her own views on being a wife.

Readers who bought the book were unaware that Margaret herself was extremely ill, with a recurrence, in 2007, of the cancer she had thought beaten twenty years earlier. Silently, it had invaded her bones, particularly her spine, and the lining of her lung. This was secondary breast cancer and could not be cured, though it could be kept in check by radiotherapy and hormonal drug therapy. For a time Margaret was unable to write, unable even to walk unaided and feared that she had written her last book. Margaret spent weeks in hospital and came home where a room on the ground floor of the house had been adapted for her.

For the first time, Margaret and Hunter were unable to travel to the Lake District for the whole summer. Margaret had physiotherapy in the same hospice where her sister-in-law had been treated, gradually progressing from crutches to independent walking. By the middle of the summer she was able to move out of the ground floor room and manage the stairs up to her bedroom and eventually to her top floor office. This was a very important and significant step. Throughout her slow recovery, Margaret began to write again, keeping it secret even from her husband. It was very hard work because she still felt very tired. Used to being able to write ten pages a day, now she found her pen 'crawling hesitantly over one mere page in three hours'. She felt that much of what she was writing was 'halting, lame stuff', but whether what she was writing was going to be publishable didn't matter. It was, she said, all about the process.[5]

There were also worries about Hunter's health, after a mysterious collapse on the beach during a family holiday. Hunter was still working at full stretch, with a string of best-sellers. He was the ghostwriter behind biographies of Wayne Rooney and Paul Gascoigne and - in a sudden switch from football to politics - John Prescott. There were also children's books, a biography of Alfred Wainwright, and a parallel career as a columnist and broadcaster. He established The Lakeland Book of the Year Awards, a much sought after regional prize, and was awarded an OBE for services to literature. Around the time of Margaret's diagnosis, Hunter had just been approached by the family of John Lennon to edit John's letters for a substantial fee. His earnings had consistently outstripped hers. When Margaret confessed in *Good Wives* that she had always considered Hunter's work more important than her own, it was perhaps something to do with earning power. Hunter had always been at the commercial end of the curve and Margaret at the literary end. It is a sad statistic that women's work is almost always valued less because they earn less. Readers might be surprised to find that Margaret's sales figures are substantial, but not always in the top league.

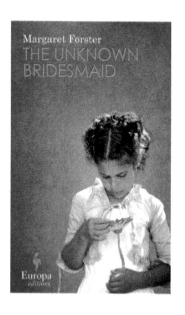

When she became ill, Margaret had been 140 pages into another novel called *The Unknown Bridesmaid*. When she returned to it, she found that she could no longer remember the details of the plot, or what her intentions had been for the characters. It had been written from two different points of view, but now 'I couldn't understand either of them'. Margaret tore it up and began again, with only the 'tiny seed' of the original idea.[6]

Margaret became well enough to return to her Cumbrian summer home and go for long walks in the fells. But in the summer of 2010, a recurrence of the cancer in her spine, which affected her right arm, meant the postponement of the novel yet again. 'The poor *Unknown Bridesmaid* looked like remaining unknown for ever.'[7] But it was eventually finished and published in 2013, though Margaret was never entirely satisfied with it. She wrote, in a note to her editor, that she had expected to have had the manuscript returned to her with 'see me' written all over it, like one of her Oxford essays that hadn't made the grade.

The novel is a 'psychological detective story', which features another of Margaret's deeply flawed heroines, Julia, who is anti-social to the point of being almost autistic. Her problems can be traced back to her childhood, the absence of her father and a strange event connected with the death of her cousin's baby. The story opens with a small child being coaxed to play with a doll. The adult Julia is a child psychiatrist, observing and assessing the children who are referred to her through social services and the criminal justice system. A *Guardian* reviewer commented that 'we are drawn ineluctably into something darker that we sense is always floating just beneath the surface of what Julia chooses to tell us'.[8]

Julia's case studies are interspersed with sections of her own 'back-story'. In particular, the time when she was eight years old and invited to be a bridesmaid at her cousin's wedding. We get a glimpse of Julia's penny-pinching, joyless mother, the anticipation of the occasion and then the anticlimax when the wedding doesn't live up to Julia's expectations. The dress is cream, not pink and it's too small for her. The eight year old child feels out of place. 'She felt she was distorted, though she didn't know if this was the fault of the tight dress or the mirror. Whatever the reason, she felt miserable.' Things don't get any better.

The bridegroom gives Julia a small gift to be given to the bride after the ceremony, but Julia has no idea what she ought to do with it and eventually forgets. As a child Julia is socially awkward, and difficult to the point where we begin to suspect that something is wrong. She has destructive impulses she can't always control. Julia grows up with that canker still inside her, forcing her to repeat the pattern that has formed her. As an adult, Julia observes that 'everything, in every person's life, led back to childhood, a truism which she'd found could not be stressed enough'. In her adult professional life, Julia often identifies the mother as the source of the child's problems. We eventually realise that Julia is a very unreliable narrator of her own story.

Julia is another of Margaret's prickly, unyielding female characters, caught up in their own interior worlds, unable to relate to other people, stubborn and anti-social. Unlike her cousin Iris, the popular bride, Julia is not a likeable person either as a child or as an adult. The sections of case study seem to be designed to help us understand the psychology of Julia's childhood self and the events that follow. Although some reviewers liked them, many readers found them repetitive and I, personally, would have preferred a more in depth exploration of Julia's emotional life, which Margaret - as author - stands resolutely outside, looking in.

Margaret's novels are full of characters like Julia; independent, aloof, proud to make their own way in life without depending on anyone else. Characters who say 'anyway, I'm managing,' even when they're clearly not; characters intent on 'keeping the world away'. The reader inevitably asks, Why? What is it about these prickly, anti-social individuals that fascinates the novelist? Is it because they reflect something in her own character that she doesn't completely understand?

~~~~~~~~~~~~~~~~~~~

19

The publicity photographs that accompanied interviews and articles to publicise *The Unknown Bridesmaid* showed a gaunt, grey-haired figure, and they shocked many people. The public had been completely unaware of Margaret's fight with cancer. She abandoned her characteristic privacy and described it for the first time in her new memoir *My Life in Houses*, published in 2014 - exactly fifty years since the publication of her first novel. Many people (myself included) believe that Margaret's memoirs are her best writing. In them she speaks directly to the reader without the need to filter ideas through fictional characters. *Hidden Lives*, *Precious Lives* and *Good Wives* dealt with family history, relationships and marriage. *My Life in Houses* tells the story of Margaret's own life using the framework of the houses that she has lived in. The idea for the book came to her when she was reading Leonard Woolf's autobiography *Downhill All the Way*. When she read what he had to say about houses and how they shape our lives, Margaret began to think about her own. 'The house determines the day-to-day, minute-to-minute quality, colour, atmosphere, pace of one's life,' Woolf observed. 'It is the framework of what one does, of what one can do, of one's relations with people. . . looking back on my life, I tend to see it divided into sections which are determined by the houses in which I have lived'.[1] And that is the structure that Margaret adopts for her memoir.

She admitted in an interview that she had kept diaries since she was ten years old - not every year, but enough to cover her life in some detail. These were a wonderful resource for autobiography, because Margaret could pin down exact dates for the events she was writing about and a level of practical detail that would not otherwise have been remembered. They also provided a window into the mind of the young girl who grew up in such different circumstances. When we look back at our childhood and adolescence most of us are tempted to edit the recollections - time alters perspective and memory is treacherous. Diaries provide firm ground from which to work.

As a teenager, Margaret admitted that she was obsessed with houses, longing to move from the cramped council house she lived in with her parents and two siblings. She fantasised about living in some of the beautiful houses she walked past, or glimpsed from the bus. Margaret's only escape was into her imagination, 'fantasising, or daydreaming, was how I lived my life'.[2] She shared a room and a bed with her sister and longed for a room of her own. She was too ashamed to invite friends home from school.

The word 'home' is at the very centre of the book. When Margaret and Hunter first married they stretched their budget as far it would go to buy a house in north London near, but on the 'wrong side' of Hampstead Heath. Later, when both were earning a substantial income from books, they could have afforded to move to the location they had both dreamed of when they were newly married. But Margaret found that she didn't want to do so and carried on living in the same house. The feeling of security and privacy it gave her was very important. 'My house is like a garment, made to my exact measurements, draped around me in the way I like.' It was the only place where she felt totally 'comfortable and relaxed'.[3]

My Life in Houses was never meant to be a cancer memoir. Margaret was adamant that it was to be purely about houses. In an interview for Foyles bookshop in London she said that she was tired of cancer memoirs 'worthy though they are', and admitted that 'I had to force myself to write anything at all about cancer'.[4] But, inevitably, Margaret found that she had to write about it; cancer, she realised, had changed the meaning of the house for her. It became a refuge, the only place she felt safe, and its familiar rooms an enormous pleasure and comfort. With almost brutal stoicism, she also wrote about the future she faced within its walls. One day, she acknowledged, the drug treatment would cease to be effective and she would have to make the decision whether to die at home or in a hospice. Her practical analysis of the pros and cons is almost shocking in its candour.

In the words of a reviewer, *My Life in Houses* is 'a beautiful, wise, profoundly moving book'.[5] But not everyone found it so. One reviewer called it 'a memoir of upwardly mobile living' and felt that the book was marred by 'a sense of entitlement'. The *Sunday Times* felt that Margaret talked too much about property renovation and too little about her own life. The modern publishing arena demands a great deal from autobiography these days, blood on the carpet and drama in the bedroom at the very least. They were never going to get that from Margaret Forster. This is a 'gentle' book, which another reviewer compared to a chat with a very intelligent woman over a cup of tea.

Margaret claimed not to care what happened to

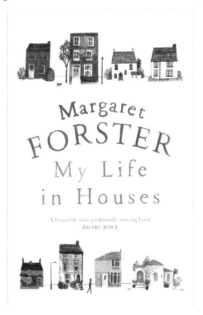

her books once they were published. They went out into the world and had to fend for themselves while she simply got on with the next. It was the writing of them that gave her joy. When writing a novel, she said that she aimed for something fictional that resembled reality as closely as possible, sometimes sacrificing form for credibility. 'I don't like books where everything is tied up. When I'm writing a novel it's real to me at the time and there are always loose ends in reality.'[6] Many readers like this. One of them remarks in an online review that 'Reading her books is a little like overhearing conversations on a bus, snatches of other people lives, with no definite conclusions.'[7]

Margaret had outstanding success as a writer that brought steady financial rewards. She had no illusions about the value of this - observing that writing in a garret wasn't necessarily a good thing. Like Virginia Woolf she recommended a room of one's own and a secure income to maximise creativity. 'I have never undervalued money. People who say money doesn't matter or bring you happiness are talking rubbish! It brings you ENORMOUS happiness!'[8] She once referred to herself as 'a very minor novelist' and, when asked by the BBC's Sue Lawley what her assessment of her own work would be, replied, 'she nearly gets there but doesn't quite'.

She was always self-deprecating. 'I certainly don't look at anything I've written as any kind of life's work,' Margaret told another interviewer sharply, 'I mean, for goodness sake, if one thing being Cumbrian gives you it's keeping your feet on the ground and getting things in context. In Carlisle we used to say that people were lost if they fancied themselves. I don't think I could ever get lost or fancy myself.' [9]

Margaret's values and her attitude to life were rooted in her upbringing in that crowded council house in Carlisle; the teenage longing for a better life and the struggle to realise those early personal ambitions that formed her character. The considerable success she enjoyed didn't change her, which is a rare quality. And, even though legendary figures such as the Beatles were regular visitors to her kitchen table, she never embraced celebrity culture. Unlike most of her contemporaries she lived in the same house for fifty years and was married to the same man for even longer. She used to tell anyone who asked that this was simply 'luck', but it wasn't just that. Something more had to be at work; tenacity, strength of will, commitment, passion, staying-power - all the qualities she appeared to value in the characters she put into her books and certainly ones that characterised the novelist herself.

Margaret's writing career evidenced the same commitment as her private life and she continued to write and publish a wide variety of books through all the challenges and upheavals that have taken place in publishing over the last five decades - changes that have defeated many other authors. Her courage and determination while living under the shadow of a cancer diagnosis were also remarkable. In Cumbria they call it 'northern grit'!

~~~~~~~~~~~~~~~~~~~~

20

In 2014 Hunter Davies was given an OBE in the 2014 Birthday Honours list for services to literature. Margaret did not approve. 'You're not going to accept it,' she said when he told her. And she added that if it had been a knighthood she would have divorced him. A firm socialist, she always declined any honours herself.

Margaret's last books were written under challenging conditions. The cancer in her bones, particularly her spine, spread relentlessly and required more and more medical intervention to slow its progress. Margaret became less and less mobile and summers at Loweswater had to be abandoned so that she could be nearer to her doctors. But, if her body was diminished, her spirit was as feisty as ever. She began another novel, set this time openly in Cumbria.

How to Measure a Cow is set in the Barrow in Furness and Ulverston area, in the shadow of the nuclear submarine works. The characters are classic Forster. The heroine, Sarah Scott aka Tara Fraser, is a prickly, reclusive, not particularly likeable, figure, paired with one of Margaret's indomitable old ladies. There are echoes of Maudie Tipstaff and Mrs McKay in the curious, curtain-twitching Nancy. The novel opens with a mystery. A young woman moves into a terraced house in the street, opposite Nancy's window.

'Sarah' doesn't socialise with anyone or give away any personal details and she is visited by a person whose job it is to supervise what is obviously a new identity. Who is she? Why is she here? What has Tara Fraser done? The plot unwinds cleverly until about two thirds of the way through the book, when sud-

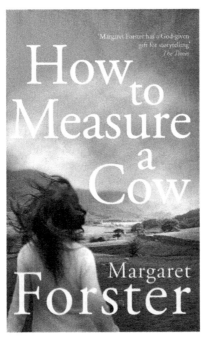

denly there is a shift in the quality of the narrative. I was, like some other readers, disappointed by the ending.

Forster fans were happy with the book overall but with some qualifications. "Forster's great gift was for illuminating the details of ordinary lives - the facades we show the outside world and our true natures within," one reviewer wrote, adding that however, "much is left unsaid and unexplained for readers to deduce for themselves". Others commented on inconsistencies, particularly in Tara/Sarah's finances, others on the unsatisfactory ending. "I did enjoy the book, but I was left at the end feeling that it should have taken me somewhere ... but it didn't!"[1]

What many readers didn't know was that Margaret was again desperately ill when she wrote the novel, which was published posthumously. The cancer had advanced through her spine. She was losing the use of her legs and her right hand – the hand she used to write with. Although her mind remained clear, her physical ability to write and to edit was curtailed. She wrote very slowly, in a difficult left-handed script, and the effort quickly exhausted her.

In January of 2015 she decided to move to the Marie Curie hospice in Hampstead. She was now totally paralysed from the waist down and realised that she was dying. Margaret had always thought that she would want to die at home, in the house she loved so much in Boscastle Road. But now that the time had come she made a different decision, putting the needs of others before her own. 'It would be awful for Hunter. He could never cope,' she told Valerie Grove. She had a beautiful room at the hospice, filled with flowers, and her family were frequent visitors. Margaret kept her sense of humour to the end, telling a friend, three days before she died, that she couldn't ever go home now because, 'Hunter has bought a MICROWAVE!'[2]

Margaret died on the 8th February. Her daughter Caitlin announced the news in a tweet; 'our lovely mum Margaret Forster died this morning', adding, 'Her books will live on.' Margaret was cremated a few days later at the Golders Green Crematorium in a private ceremony attended by family and close friends, including fellow Cumbrian Melvyn Bragg and her publisher Carmen Callil. A devastated Hunter chose the Beatles' song 'And I Love Her' for the service. Everyone was invited back to Boscastle Road afterwards for 'tea and buns', in a low-key celebration that Margaret would have approved. 'She hated to be noticed,' Hunter said. Margaret and Hunter had been together for sixty years, since Margaret was seventeen.

Initially, Hunter's busy literary life in London, his newspaper columns and commissioned books, kept him from brooding too much on Margaret's death. 'I have not had time to mope, moan or mourn,' he wrote. But in their Lake District house at Loweswater it was a different matter. The quiet, isolated house was too full of memories and Margaret's absence too apparent. He decided that he couldn't bear to live there alone. The house was put on the market in July 2015 and quickly sold. All the possessions that it contained went either to the children or to the auction houses, including all his football memorabilia. He now lives all the year round at their house in Boscastle Road and his humorous memoir of his life with

Margaret Forster was published in April 2016, titled, with typical Hunter wit, *The Co-op's Got Bananas: A Memoir of Growing up in the Post War North*. Theirs was a unique partnership. Margaret, he says, will always be with him.

~~~~~~~~~~~~~~~~~~~~~~~

CHRONOLOGY

* indicates non-fiction

Dames' Delight   1964
Georgy Girl   1965
The Bogeyman   1965
The Travels of Maudie Tipstaff   1967
The Park   1968
Miss Owen-Owen is at Home 1969
Fenella Phizackerley 1970
Mr Bone's Retreat   1971
*The Rash Adventurer: The Rise and
 Fall of Charles Edward Stuart   1973
The Seduction of Mrs Pendlebury   1974
*Thackeray   1978
Mother, can you hear me?   1979
The Bride of Lowther Fell   1980
Marital Rites 1981
*Significant Sisters   1984
Private Papers   1986
*Elizabeth Barrett Browning   1988
* Elizabeth Barrett Browning,   Selected Poems
 (Editor)   1988

Have the Men had Enough? 1989
Lady's Maid   1990
The Battle for Christabel   1991
*Daphne Du Maurier   1993
Mothers'Boys   1994
*Hidden Lives   1995
Shadow Baby   1996
*Rich Desserts and Captain Thin   1997
*Precious Lives   1998
The Memory Box   1999
*Good Wives?   2001
Diary of an Ordinary Woman   2003
Is there anything you Want?   2005
Keeping the World Away   2006
Over 2006
Isa and May 2009
The Unknown Bridesmaid   2013
*My Life in Houses   2014
How to Measure a Cow 2015

ENDNOTES

Unless otherwise stated, page references are to the Penguin paperback editions of the books.

Introduction
1. *Guardian Review*, 10th March, 2013
2. Helen Berry - *Guardian*, 21.9.02
3. Heather Mallick -- Toronto Sun

Chapter 1
1. *Hidden Lives*,   Ch VI, p.122
2. *Hidden Lives.* Ch VIII p. 151
3. *Hidden Lives* Ch VIII p 155
4. bid
5. Ibid
6. Hidden Lives Ch X, p.183
7. Ibid
8. *Hidden Lives* Ch XIII, p. 225
9. *Hidden Lives* Ch. XIV, p.229

Chapter 2
1. *Strong Lad wanted for Strong Lass*, Bookcase, Carlisle, 2004, p.96
2. Ibid. p.113
3. *Good Wives*, Reflections on Jennie Lee, p.291
4. *Hidden Lives* Ch XV, p 246.
5. *Dames' Delight*, Hardback   p.18
6. Ibid. Hardback p.154
7. Ibid. p.176
8. Ibid.   p.178
9. Ibid. p.158

10. Ibid. final chapter.

Chapter 3

1. *Strong Lad wanted for Strong Lass*, Bookcase, Carlisle, 2004, p.119
2. http://www.dailymail.co.uk/home/books/a article-478541/Loss-An-Interview-Margaret-Forster.html
3. *Hidden Lives*, Ch XVI, p.262
4. *Georgy Girl*, Hardback, Ch.3.
5. http://www.dailymail.co.uk/home/books/article-69719/Q-A-Margaret-Forster.html
6. Desert Island Discs, 4th December 1994
7. http://www.randomhousesites.co.uk/readersgroup/ printguide.htm?command=Search&db=/catalog/ main.txt&eqisbndata=0099496860

Chapter 4

1. *Precious Lives*, Vintage, p.212, Ch. VIII.
2. *Hidden Lives,* Ch. XVI, p 264.
3. *Hidden Lives,* Ch. XVI, p. 265.
4. *Hidden Lives,* Ch. XVI, p. 264.

Chapter 5

1. *Maudie Tipstaff,* Hardback, pt. 3, ch 5.
2. *Maudie Tipstaff* , Hardback, pt. 3,   ch.5
3. Ibid. pt. 3, ch 4.

Chapter 6

1. *The Rash Adventurer,* Hardback, Preface, p.xiii.
2.Ibid. p.xiv.
3. Ibid. p. xv.
4. *The Rash Adventurer,* Hardback, Introduction, pp.4-5.

5. Ibid. p.155.
6. Ibid. p.308.
7. My Life in Houses, p.175
8. Ibid.
9. Ibid.p.179
10. *Thackeray,* Introduction
11. Ibid.

Chapter 7
1. *My Life in Houses,* p.186
2. Ibid.p.189
3. Ibid. p.189
4. Ibid. p.191
5. Significant Sisters, Introduction p. 10
6. Ibid. Conclusion p.321
7. Ibid. Introduction p.10
8. *Mother, can you hear me?* Ch IV, p. 62 & Ch VI, p.87
9. Ibid. Ch XIII, p.205

Chapter 8
1. '*Writers' Rooms*', The Guardian, 18th April, 2008.
2. https://www.penguin.co.uk/articles/on-writing/times-and-life/2016/mar/remembering-margaret-forster/#hzv7ahPw4TjkRzAZ.99
3. Hunter Davies, Evening Standard, February, 2016.
4. *Cumbria Life,* 1999, http://www.alanair.co.uk/images/margaretforster.pdf
5. *Good Wives,* Reflections on Fanny Stevenson, hardback, p.195
6. Cumbria Life, 1999, http://www.alanair.co.uk/images/margaretforster.pdf
7. Desert Island Discs, 4th December, 1994.

8. Ibid.
9. Ibid.

Chapter 9
1. http://www.dk.com/static/rguides/uk/
   readers6_0140284117.html
2. Desert Island Discs, 4th December, 1994.
3. Ibid.
4. *Elizabeth Barrett Browning*, paperback, p.xiii
5. Ibid. p.xiv
6. *Selected Poems of Elizabeth Barrett Browning*,
   hardback, p.xvii
7. Kenyon, Frederic G., ed. The Letters of Elizabeth
   Barrett Browning. 2 vols. London: Smith, Elder
   & Co., 1897. Vol I, p.231.

Chapter 10
1. *Lady's Maid*, paperback, p.184
2. A Northern Lass in NW5, Valerie Grove, *New
Statesman*, 11th March 2016
3. *Daphne du Maurier* Acknowledgements p. xiv
4. http://www.dailymail.co.uk/home/books/
   article-478541/Loss-An-Interview-Margaret-
   Forster.html
5. http://www.randomhousesites.co.uk/readersgroup/
   printguide.htm?command=Search&db=/catalog/
   main.txt&eqisbndata=0099496860

Chapter 11
1. Nominated as 'Book of the Year' nine times in
   1995
2. *Cumbria Life,* 1999, http://www.alanair.co.uk/
   images/margaretforster.pdf
3. *Hidden Lives,* Ch XIX p.304

4. *Hidden Lives,* Author's Note p.308

Chapter 12
1. *The Memory Box,* Amazon.co.uk
2. http://www.dailymail.co.uk/home/books/article-69719/Q-A-Margaret-Forster.html
3. http://www.dk.com/static/rguides/uk/readers6_0140284117.html
4. http://blog.hellomagazine.com/offtheshelf/tag/caitlin-davies
5. http://www.telegraph.co.uk/culture/books/3644305/A-hot-sun-and-a-chill-wind.html

Chapter 13
1. Precious Lives, Vintage Ch VI, p.133
2. Ibid. Ch V, p.124
3. Ibid. Prologue, p.14
4. Ibid. Ch VIII, p.194
5. Ibid. Ch VIII, p.198

Chapter 14
1. *Cumbria Life,* 1999, http://www.alanair.co.uk/images/margaretforster.pdf
2. *Good Wives,* Prologue, hardback p.8
3. Ibid
4. *Good Wives*, Reflections on Mary Livingstone, hardback p.102
5. Daily Mail interview, http://www.dailymail.co.uk/home/books/article-478541/Loss-An-Interview-Margaret-Forster.html
6. *Good Wives*, Reflections on Mary Livingstone, hardback p.104
7. *Mother, can you hear me?* Ch 15, p.233
8. *Good Wives,* Reflections on Mary Livingstone,

hardback p.105

9. *Good Wives,* Reflections on Jennie Lee, hardback, p.297
10. Ibid. p.310
11. Ibid. p.311

Chapter 15
1. *Diary of an Ordinary Woman*, hardback, p.1
2. http://readersplace.co.uk/view-reading-guide/ diary-of-an-ordinary-woman/
3. *Diary of an Ordinary Woman,* hardback, p.7
4. http://readersplace.co.uk/view-reading-guide/ diary-of-an-ordinary-woman/
5. *Diary of an Ordinary Woman,* hardback, p.7
6. www.guardian.co.uk/books/2003/apr/19/ featuresreviews.guardianreview14

Ch 16
1. Caitlin Davies, *A Place of Reeds,* Simon & Schuster UK Ltd, 2005
2. *Is There Anything You Want?* Paperback, p.28
3. https://www.penguin.co.uk/articles/on-writing/ times-and-life/2016/mar/remembering-margaret-forster/#hzv7ahPw4TjkRzAZ.99
4. http://www.guardian.co.uk/books/2005/jan/29/ featuresreviews.guardianreview15
5. www.amazon.co.uk

Ch 17
1. Simon Humphreys, the Mail on Sunday, 9th April, 2006.
2. Susann Cokal, http://www.nytimes.com/2007/07/29/books/review/Cokal-t.html
3. Alexis Burling, http://www.bookreporter.com/

reviews/keeping-the-world-away
4. *BP Portrait Award 2006*, National Portrait
Gallery,   London, 2002, p.8
5. BP Portrait Award 2006, pp.12/13

Ch 18

1. *Over,* paperback, p.80
2. *Over,* paperback, p.2
3. http://www.dailymail.co.uk/home/books/
   article-478541/Loss-An-Interview-Margaret-
   Forster.html
4. http://www.dailymail.co.uk/home/books/
   article-478541/Loss-An-Interview-Margaret-
   Forster.html
5 *My Life in Houses*, p.255
6. Ibid.
7. Ibid. p.259
8. *Guardian,* 10th March 2013

Ch 19

1. Leonard Woolf, D*ownhill All the Way:* An
   Autobiography of the Years 1919-1939, 1967
2. *My Life in Houses,* p.30
3.Ibid. p.264
4. http://www.foyles.co.uk/Margaret-Forster
5. *Guardian,* Rachel Cooke, 9th November, 2014
6. http://www.dailymail.co.uk/home/books/article-
69719/Q-A-Margaret-Forster.html
7. Veronica - Goodreads.com
8. *Cumbria Life,* 1999, http://www.alanair.co.uk/
images/margaretforster.pdf
9. *Cumbria Life,* 1999, http://www.alanair.co.uk/
images/margaretforster.pdf

Ch 20

1. *Amazon Reader's Reviews*
2. Valerie Grove. *New Statesman,* 11th March 2015

More Books By Kathleen Jones

Biography
Margaret Cavendish: A Glorious Fame, the Life of the Duchess of Newcastle, Bloomsbury Publishing & The Book Mill E-book
Christina Rossetti: Learning not to be First, Oxford University Press & The Book Milll E-book
A Passionate Sisterhood: The Sisters, Wives and Daughter of the Lake Poets, Virago & The Book Mill E-book
Catherine Cookson: The Biography, Times Warner
Seeking Catherine Cookson's Da, Constable Robinson
Katherine Mansfield: The Storyteller, Penguin NZ, Edinburgh University Press
Margaret Forster: A Life in Books, The Bookmill E-book
Norman Nicholson: The Whispering Poet, The Book Mill

Fiction
Three and Other Stories, The Book Mill E-book
The Sun's Companion, The Book Mill
The Centauress, The Book Mill

Non Fiction
Travelling to the Edge of the World , The Book Mill

Poetry
Unwritten Lives, Redbeck Press
Not Saying Goodbye at Gate 21, Templar Poetry

As Kate Gordon
An Alternative Guide to Weddings
An Alternative Guide to Baptism and Baby-naming
An Alternative Guide to Funerals

Lightning Source UK Ltd.
Milton Keynes UK
UKOW06f1619190417
299426UK00011B/27/P